ZOMBIE SURVIVAL PUZZLES

THIS IS A CARLTON BOOK

Published by Carlton Books Ltd
20 Mortimer Street
London W1T 3JW

A CIP catalogue for this book is available from the
British Library.

Design and illustrations: WildPixel Ltd
Managing art editor: Stephen Cary
Project editor: Chris Mitchell
Puzzle checking: Tim Dedopulos
Production: Yael Steinitz

ISBN 978-1-78097-989-2

Printed in Dubai

10 9 8 7 6 5 4 3 2 1

ZOMBIE SURVIVAL PUZZLES

JASON WARD

CARLTON
BOOKS

CONTENTS

INTRODUCTION 10

SEASON 1: WALKERS 12

TURN BACK: PART 1 14

TURN BACK: PART 2 15

TURN BACK: PART 3 16

SUPPLY RUNNER RUNNING 17

FURTHER DOWN 18

A PICK OF BAD CHOICES 19

SOMETHING HIDDEN 20

NUMBERED DAYS 21

THE QUIZZING DEAD SEASON 1-EASY. 22

THE QUIZZING DEAD SEASON 2-HARD 23

SEASON 2: LURKERS 24

THE SCENIC ROUTE: PART 1. 26

THE SCENIC ROUTE: PART 2 27

THE SCENIC ROUTE: PART 3 28

DEAD AIM 29

HITTING THE BOTTLE: PART 1. 30

HITTING THE BOTTLE: PART 2 31

TRACKING GHOSTS 32

SCHOOL ORIENTATION 33

HEALTH PROBLEMS 34

THE QUIZZING DEAD SEASON 2-EASY 35

THE QUIZZING DEAD SEASON 2-HARD 36

MODERN ROMANCE: PART 1 37

MODERN ROMANCE: PART 2. 38

UNSAFE SAFE CRACKING. 39

THE LAST FARM: PART 1. 40

THE LAST FARM: PART 2. 41

THE LAST FARM: PART 3. 42

BAD COP 43

SPOT THE DIFFERENCE 44

COUNTING THE DEAD. 46

SEASON 3: BITERS 48

SOLITARY CONFINEMENT: PART 1 50
SOLITARY CONFINEMENT: PART 2 51
SOLITARY CONFINEMENT: PART 3 52
SOLITARY CONFINEMENT: PART 4 53
SOMETHING HIDDEN 2 54
A DEATH SENTENCE. 55
THE BIG QUESTION 56
MISSING THE TRAIN 57
UNSAFE SAFE CRACKING 2 58
THE QUIZZING DEAD SEASON 3-EASY 59
THE QUIZZING DEAD SEASON 3-HARD 60
THE FESTIVITIES: PART 1. 61
THE FESTIVITIES: PART 2 62
THE FESTIVITIES: PART 3 63
ALARMED. 64
THE SLOW ROAD. 65
NEW FRIENDS. 66
DEAD AIM 2 67
PILLOW PROBLEMS: PART 1 68
PILLOW PROBLEMS: PART 2 69

SEASON 4: SKIN EATERS 70

THE GRAVEYARD SHIFT. 72
RETROSPECTIVELY DISCONCERTING. 73
SPOT THE DIFFERENCE 2. 74
THREE QUESTIONS: PART 1 76
THREE QUESTIONS: PART 2 77
THREE QUESTIONS: PART 3 78
SOMETHING HIDDEN 3 79
HIS BEST SELF 80
UNSAFE SAFE CRACKING 3 81
THE QUIZZING DEAD SEASON 4-EASY 82
THE QUIZZING DEAD SEASON 4-HARD 83
SURVIVOR'S GUILT 84
BORED GAME. 85

JACKSONVILLE, BEFORE 86

END OF THE LINE 87

SEASON 5: ROAMERS 88

HOLDING A TORCH 90

A WAYS AWAY: PART 1 91

A WAYS AWAY: PART 2 92

A WAYS AWAY: PART 3 93

WILD CANNIBAL YOUTH 94

MAKING AN EXIT 95

UNSAFE SAFE-CRACKING 4 96

1,434 MILES: PART 1 97

1,434 MILES: PART 2 98

1,434 MILES: PART 3 99

1,434 MILES: PART 4 100

SLABTOWN 101

ORDERLY ORDERLIES 102

STICKY FINGERS 103

THE QUIZZING DEAD SEASON 5-EASY 104

THE QUIZZING DEAD SEASON 5-HARD 105

BLOODY KIDS: PART 1 106

BLOODY KIDS: PART 2 107

DEAD AIM 3 108

HOLED UP 109

A CLEAR OUT 110

SOMETHING HIDDEN 4 111

TENDING THE FLOCK: PART 1 112

TENDING THE FLOCK: PART 2 113

TENDING THE FLOCK: PART 3 114

SEASON 6: COLD BODIES 116

THE NEW WORLD 118

LUCK RUNNING LOW: PART 1 119

LUCK RUNNING LOW: PART 2 120

WOLVES NOT FAR: PART 1 121

WOLVES NOT FAR: PART 2 122

WOLVES NOT FAR: PART 3 123

WOLVES NOT FAR: PART 4 124

UNSAFE SAFE CRACKING 5 125

COURTING TROUBLE 126

THE QUIZZING DEAD SEASON 6-EASY 127

THE QUIZZING DEAD SEASON 6-HARD 128

THE WRONG MAN: PART 1 129

THE WRONG MAN: PART 2 130

THE WRONG MAN: PART 3 131

SPOT THE DIFFERENCE 3 132

A LIFE OR DEATH DECISION 134

SAFE PASSAGE: PART 1 135

SAFE PASSAGE: PART 2 136

SAFE PASSAGE: PART 3 137

SOMETHING HIDDEN 5 138

SEASON 7: ROTTERS 140

A SLIP OF PAPER 142

DEAD AIM 4 143

THE SMALL HOURS 144

4:30 TO ALEXANDRIA 145

UNSAFE SAFE CRACKING 6 146

THE WELL: PART 1 147

THE WELL: PART 2 148

THE WELL: PART 3 149

THE WELL: PART 4 150

THE QUIZZING DEAD SEASON 7-EASY 151

THE QUIZZING DEAD SEASON 7-HARD 152

AN ABSENT FATHER 153

STRANGE CURRENCIES 154

WARMONGERING 155

THE HOPEFUL DEPUTY: PART 1 156

THE HOPEFUL DEPUTY: PART 2 157

THE SAVIOUR: PART 1 158

THE SAVIOUR: PART 2 159

THE SAVIOUR: PART 3 160

KEEP GOING 161

ANSWERS 162

He had screamed, and wept, and even pulled over briefly to howl his fists into the hot, unyielding asphalt, but Rick Grimes had never felt so broken as when he reached for his sedan's turn signal.

Who was he planning to indicate to? Not only were there no moving vehicles on the road but those he could see were abandoned, upside down, smashed up. There was no need to announce his movements to anyone and yet at every corner his right fingers went straight for that signal.

As a police officer, Rick had spent more of his days inside cars than outside them, he supposed. His whole adult life, instinctively touching a switch, so now what?

Join Rick Grimes and his companions as they travel through a world torn apart. Solve these puzzles to survive. Fail, and you too might find yourself torn apart... or worse.

SEASON 1

WALKERS

PART 1

At the turn for the highway, a warning scrawled on a hung bedsheet read **"NOT THIS WAY"** and Rick heeded its instruction.

There was even more advice ahead. He soon found himself at an intersection, where someone had spray-painted **"SAFETY HERE, OR ELSE YOU SHOULD GO RIGHT"** on the road sign for the left path. The repurposed sign for the right path, meanwhile, just stated **"DEAD ON HIGHWAY"**.

It had clearly been days since the notices were written, so Rick knew that at least one of them had now to be false.

Q Should he go left, right, or brave the highway?

Walkers

14

Solution on page 164

PART 2

There were so many obstacles littering the road that Rick had to pay constant attention, and yet he couldn't bear to look.

Swerving at the last moment, he almost crashed trying to avoid the sight of a blackened school bus. Its windows were obscured by blood and the name on the side was familiar. He'd given a talk there once, about strangers and personal safety. Nice kids.

FUEL

The sadness just sat there, in his stomach. Rick glanced at the dashboard. He found that fear was a mildly effective distraction: the alleged refugee camp stood 175 miles away from the police station, and the fuel gauge was continuing its plunge towards E. He did some anxious calculations. Navigating the grim tangle of vehicles meant the car could only travel at a steady 30mph, and it was station protocol for the police interceptors – which made 20 miles per gallon – to be stocked with exactly 10 gallons of fuel. However, there was an apparent leak somewhere as, on top of its standard usage, the tank was losing gas at a rate of half a gallon per hour.

Q Could Rick make it to the camp before he ran out of gas?

03 TURN BACK

PART 3

↓ ATLANTA ↓

They loped towards Atlanta and, for a moment, Rick was almost at peace. If it was possible to ride a horse on an afternoon as fine as this, maybe there was hope. The road stretched on ahead. People had died in once-un-imaginable horror and there was worse to come, but that wasn't the end of the story. He would find Lori and Carl – he knew it. The world still held the means for joy.

Rick thought about the first time he rode a horse, and how his father calmed his nerves by asking riddles. At the time, he had been embarrassed – mortified even – and now he wished he could recall even a single one. They were gone, never to return.

And then he remembered:

"Brown I am and much admired, many horses have I tried;
Tire a horse and worry a man, tell me this riddle if you can."

Walkers

16

Solution on page 164

"Typical," Glenn muttered to himself, as if sensing that it soon would be. Shane had proclaimed a hunch that there might be ammo in a nearby sporting-goods store, so who better to investigate than Glenn, rather than the person who actually had the idea?

Help Glenn find his way to the store.

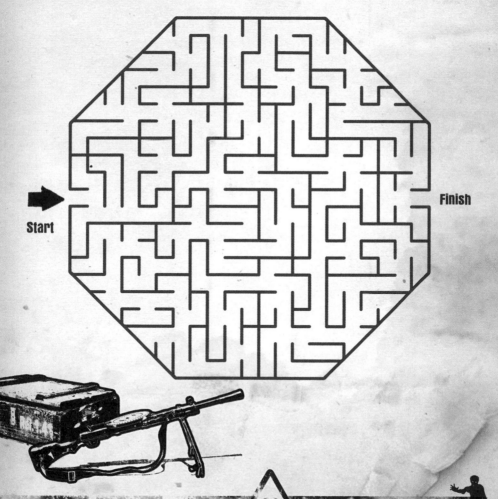

Finish

Start

Jim couldn't remember his dream, much less comprehend it. All he knew was that he woke up with the compulsion to dig a series of holes. The baking Georgia sun made hard work of the job and the concerned looks of the others were putting him on edge, but he couldn't stop himself. It didn't feel good, but he understood somehow that it was correct.

As he shovelled over and over again, Jim ignored everyone who came by – Jacqui, Dale, the kids who wanted to gawk. With grim inevitability, Shane visited last, using his calm voice that meant you'd run out of chances. He even offered to help – an idea Jim weighed for a moment before deciding not to trust.

By Jim's reckoning, it'd take him about eight hours to dig six holes. If he had accepted Shane's proposal,

Q how long would it take the two of them to dig half a hole?

Walkers

18

Solution on page 166

"When do I get a gun?" Carl asked his mother, and the saddest thing about the question was that it was no longer unreasonable. Lori was only beginning to come to terms with knowing that the education she and Rick had envisioned for their son was entirely obsolete. He would have to become a different sort of person now and, if she wanted him to make it into his teens, he would need to know how to kill.

But not yet. Not today. Lori stared at the boy and tried to push the future out of her mind. Reaching for a distraction, she posed a riddle:

"Carl, you have been condemned to death. I'm sorry. This is, you understand, a grave situation. What's worse is the fact that your captor is a cruel and capricious man. Your first clue about his mania is that he doesn't stop smiling. In a false show of mercy, he allows you to decide the room in which you'll perish. One room is engulfed by a fire that never stops burning, another holds a Bengal tiger that hasn't eaten in a year, and the third is filled with his most violent soldiers."

Which room should Carl choose?

Solution on page 166

19

Walkers

What gruesome image is concealed below?

Column clues (top to bottom):

									2	8								
					5	9			4	3	2		3	4				
2	2	1	1	2	3	5	12	10	3	3	6	9	6	3	3	2	1	1

Row clues (top to bottom):

- 1
- 1 1 1
- 2 1 2
- 2 1 2
- 2 1 1
- 2 2 2
- 1 2 1
- 2 1 1
- 2 1
- 5 2
- 7 1
- 1 8
- 2 3 3
- 2 3 3
- 1 4 3
- 5 3
- 10
- 7
- 6
- 1

To reveal the picture, shade the grid's cells so that each column and row has continuous shaded blocks of the lengths indicated by the numbers at the start of that column or row, with at least one empty cell between each block.

Walkers 20 **Solution on page 167**

08 NUMBERED DAYS

Dale watched the walker's head burst and thought about dates. They were easier to think about than other things.

He wondered if the day would come when he didn't actually know what day it was. Once he'd lived by his calendar, crossing out each passing day with a big red X, but there wasn't much need for that kind of thing any more. Did anyone else even know it was a Friday? There was barely even a tomorrow. There was just now, and then.

Through the sight of his rifle he saw that the walker was now lying in a clump by the fence. Including that one, Dale had shot 30 over the past 5 days. They were growing in number at the quarry: each day he had taken out three more walkers than the one before. Unless something changed for the better, they'd soon be completely overrun. He thought, absently, about what day that might be.

Q How many walkers did Dale shoot on Monday?

09 THE QUIZZING DEAD

SEASON 1 EASY

1. WHO WROTE AND DIRECTED THE WALKING DEAD'S PILOT EPISODE AND DEVELOPED THE SHOW FOR TELEVISION?

2. WHAT IS RICK GRIMES' POSITION IN THE POLICE FORCE?

3. WHO IS THE FIRST LIVING PERSON RICK MEETS AFTER HE WAKES UP IN THE HOSPITAL?

4. WHAT ITEMS ARE MISSING AT RICK'S HOME THAT TELLS HIM LORI AND CARL ARE STILL ALIVE?

5. WHEN HE GETS TRAPPED IN A TANK, RICK IS CONTACTED BY GLENN OVER A RADIO. WHAT DOES GLENN CALL HIM?

6. WHAT DO SHANE AND CARL ATTEMPT TO CATCH AT THE QUARRY?

7. WHAT IS THE SECRET OF THE GANG THAT KIDNAPS GLENN?

8. WHO BEATS UP CAROL'S ABUSIVE HUSBAND ED?

9. WHAT DO RICK, DARYL, T-DOG AND GLENN FIND WHEN THEY RETURN TO THE DEPARTMENT-STORE ROOF?

10. WHAT INFORMATION DOES DR EDWIN JENNER SECRETLY TELL RICK BEFORE THEY SEPARATE?

Walkers

Solution on page 168

SEASON 1 HARD

1. IN THE HOSPITAL, WHAT WORDS DOES RICK FIND SPRAY-PAINTED ON A DOOR?

2. WHAT IS THE NAME OF MORGAN'S UNDEAD WIFE?

3. WHAT WEAPON DOES RICK USE TO KILL HIS FIRST WALKER?

4. WHICH FICTIONAL PART OF GEORGIA DO RICK AND LORI LIVE IN?

5. WHAT DOES RICK ENCOURAGE ANDREA TO TAKE FROM THE DEPARTMENT STORE?

6. WHAT LURES DID ANDREA AND AMY'S DAD TEACH THEM TO USE WHEN FISHING?

7. AFTER LEAVING THE QUARRY, THE GROUP HEAD FOR THE CDC. WHAT DOES CDC STAND FOR?

8. WHO IS TEST SUBJECT 19?

9. WHAT COUNTRY DOES DR JENNER SAY WAS CLOSE TO FINDING A CURE FOR THE WALKER OUTBREAK?

10. WHICH THREE MAJOR CHARACTERS FROM SEASON 1 OF THE WALKING DEAD DIDN'T APPEAR IN THE ORIGINAL COMIC SERIES?

Solution on page 169

 23

Walkers

SEASON 2

LURKERS

THE SCENIC ROUTE:

PART 1

Periodically, Shane contemplated whether it would be faster for them all to just walk to Fort Benning. They seemingly spent half of their time pushing wrecked cars out of the road and the other half trying to repair their own malfunctioning vehicles.

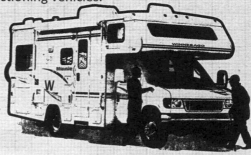

That first day, leaving behind the ruins of both the CDC and their hope for a cure, the group had only travelled 7 miles. Their progress did manage to improve gradually by 4 miles a day so that, on the day they got fatefully waylaid by a walker horde, they had driven 51 miles.

Q How long had the group been travelling for when they stopped?

Lurkers | 26 | Solution on page 169

PART 2

Surviving, as an activity, took up most of the day. Whether they were scavenging for food and supplies, killing walkers or inching towards Fort Benning, the group devoted most of their attention to the arduous feat of staying alive. Despite this, there were stretches of time when there was very little to do at all. This was especially difficult for Carl and Sophia, who were unused to a life outside of structure and school.

Their response to alternating periods of terror and boredom was to get into ridiculous spats. During one sweltering afternoon, as the adults argued over something or another, the children had a debate of their own: Carl asserted that he had killed twice as many walkers as Sophia, while Sophia claimed that she had killed twice as many walkers as Carl.

Q Both were right. How?

PART 3

When Dale told stories, it was difficult to tell whether they had actually happened to him or not. At various junctures nearly everyone in the group had wondered whether he was appropriating an anecdote in order to make a broader point. One notable incident of this occurred when he called Daryl over to the RV, where he was engaged in a losing battle with its busted radiator hose. Without waiting for a conversation to take them to the subject naturally, he began talking about his youth:

"Did I ever tell you about my brother? He was always trying to get one over on me, I think because he was older. I'll never forget the April Fools' Day he burst into my room and told me he was going to fool me as I'd never been fooled before. I was only six and couldn't decide if I was excited or petrified. I waited all day and nothing happened. It made me furious – due to my young age, I probably stamped my feet quite a bit – and I confronted him just before bed:

'So, you expected me to fool you?' he replied and I told him that I did, and then he said, 'Dale, if you expected me to fool you and I didn't, that means I did fool you.' Then he hit me on the shoulder, because he was a kind and loving brother. I've spent much of my adult life trying to parse whether he was right or not."

Did Dale's brother fool him?

Lurkers

28

Solution on page 170

14 DEAD AIM

They were running out of time. The herd had appeared from nowhere and would soon bury them all. Help Andrea kill the walkers while sparing her friends.

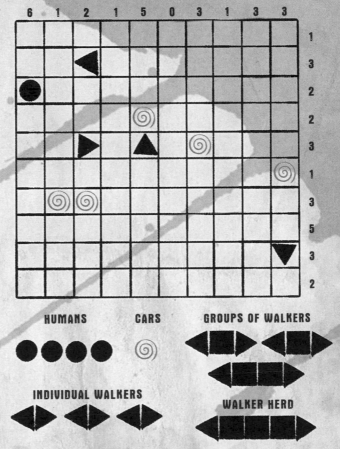

Identify the exact locations of the walkers and humans hidden in this image. All are positioned horizontally or vertically, and no one is immediately adjacent to anyone else, including diagonally. The row and column numbers indicate the total segments in their corresponding lines.

Solution on page 171

29

Lurkers

HITTING THE BOTTLE:

PART 1

There was a strange gratification to be found in shooting something that wasn't trying to eat you. The empty bottles just sat there politely, glinting in the morning sun and not attempting to murder anyone's family. It was much appreciated by everyone.

Shane, a weapons instructor since long before there was a sensible reason to fire a gun, was in his element. After showing his trainees the basics of firearm usage, he arranged a series of contests where the winner was the first person or pair to take out a designated number of bottles. To her pleasant surprise, Patricia just managed to outshoot Jimmy and Carl combined, although it was rather taxing. Patricia and Jimmy together matched Andrea and Carl, neither pair being able to shoot all of the bottles faster than the other. If Carl changed places with Jimmy, however, Andrea and Jimmy won with ease.

Q How did the four rank in terms of proficiency?

PART 2

"Let's hope the creepers dislike broken glass," Shane said, prodding at one of the shards with his shoe. The rookie sharpshooters had blasted the makeshift range until there was nothing left but a hazard for barefooted trespassers. Exhausted by the effort, they laid on their backs in the grass, ignoring the soft ringing that they could still hear. At some point the idea of retrieving more bottles was suggested but no one could muster the enthusiasm for much of anything by that point.

As if sensing the tiredness that had settled over the proceedings, Beth brought over a crate of five peaches from the garden, which was a real treat considering how zealously Hershel guarded his peach tree.

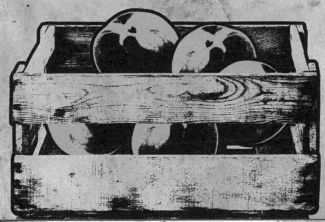

Q Without cutting any fruit, how could the peaches be divided among the five of them in such a way that one peach was left in the crate?

Solution on page 172   31   Lurkers

No one spent longer looking for Sophia than Daryl – if they hadn't eventually learned of her grisly fate, he might still be traipsing up and down a creek somewhere. It didn't matter what the personal cost was: he just couldn't give up until a job was finished. Given his family members and upbringing, he had no idea where that virtue had emerged from.

One of his more dispiriting attempts to find the missing girl came when he scaled a hill just south of the farm. Hershel had warned him that it was a difficult trek but the possibility of viewing the area from above was too useful to ignore. Daryl climbed to the summit at a rate of one and a half miles an hour but his labours were in vain: there was nothing to be seen. Powered by disappointment and gravity, the descent was much quicker, and he came down at a speed of four and a half miles per hour. Excluding the time he spent on the hilltop, it took Daryl six gruelling hours to complete the round trip.

Q How far was it to the top of the hill?

Otis stared at the map like someone was about to snatch it from him. Crouched in the school's darkened parking lot, he ignored the moans of the roamers and tried to concentrate: the respirator had to be somewhere. He wasn't going to let that boy down, let alone the man who'd kindly volunteered to help.

Start

Finish

Q How can Otis reach the medical supplies?

Solution on page 173

33

Lurkers

Perhaps it was the novelty of knowing an ill person who wasn't shortly going to turn into a walker but, following his accident, Carl was never short of visitors. As he recuperated from the gunshot wound and makeshift surgery, everyone took some time to sit with the boy and keep him entertained.

The most exciting caller was undeniably T-Dog, who came into the room brandishing three medals. He explained that, before he joined the others, he had briefly taken sanctuary in the house of an Olympic pole-vaulter who, unfortunately, hadn't survived the outbreak. He'd been carrying the athlete's medals with him ever since and might – just maybe – let the young convalescent have one. Carl's eyes lit up as he surveyed the gold, silver and bronze objects but T-Dog said there was a catch: to receive a medal, Carl would have to make a true statement and, if what he said was false, he wouldn't receive anything.

Q What did Carl say to force T-Dog to give him the gold medal?

Lurkers

34

Solution on page 174

20 THE QUIZZING DEAD

1. THE WALKING DEAD IS BASED ON THE POPULAR COMIC-BOOK SERIES WRITTEN BY WHICH AUTHOR?

2. HOW DOES LORI CRASH HER CAR?

3. WHO ACCIDENTALLY SHOOTS CARL?

4. WHAT DOES LORI ASK GLENN TO RETRIEVE WHEN HE VISITS THE PHARMACY?

5. WHO IS THE FIRST NON-WALKER HUMAN THAT DARYL KILLS?

6. WHY DOES SHANE SHAVE HIS HEAD?

7. WHAT DOES HERSHEL GIVE GLENN AS A PRESENT?

8. WHO DOES DARYL HALLUCINATE SEEING WHEN HE GETS WOUNDED BY A CROSSBOW BOLT?

9. WHERE WAS SOPHIA FOUND?

10. HOW DOES THE WALKER THAT ATTACKS DALE GET TO THE FARM?

Solution on page 174

35

Lurkers

SEASON 2 HARD

1. THE CREDITS FOR THE FIRST TWO SEASONS FEATURE THE IMAGE OF A NEWSPAPER. WHAT IS ITS HEADLINE?

2. WHICH LEGENDARY CREATURE DOES DARYL CLAIM TO HAVE ONCE SEEN WHILE SQUIRREL HUNTING?

3. WHAT IS THE NICKNAME OF HERSHEL'S HORSE?

4. WHAT ARE RICK AND CARL'S BLOOD TYPES?

5. WHAT IS T-DOG'S REAL NAME?

6. WHAT TYPE OF FLOWER DOES DARYL GIVE TO CAROL?

7. WHAT IS ON THE END OF SHANE'S NECKLACE?

8. WHAT ARE THE NAMES OF THE TWO MEN THAT RICK, HERSHEL AND GLENN ENCOUNTER IN PATTON'S BAR?

9. HOW DOES T-DOG CUT HIS ARM?

10. WHAT BOOK DOES ANDREA GIVE TO DARYL TO APOLOGISE FOR SHOOTING HIM?

PART 1

Maggie wasn't entirely sure what her type was, or if she even had one, but presumably most of the relevant candidates had perished by now anyway. She wasn't particularly troubled by this fact: in the wake of the most cataclysmic event in human history, dating was low on her list of concerns. And then she met Glenn.

There was something about him. He was smart and brave but didn't know it. He put others before himself, every time, even when it meant being lowered into a well to grapple with a bloated walker straight from a nightmare. Glenn was obviously interested too: he had somehow got the unfounded idea into his head that she liked riddles, and had been canvassing everyone for suggestions. His latest one – technically Dale's latest one – was this:

"The part of the bird that is not in the sky. Which can swim in the ocean and always stay dry."

Q What's the answer?

23 MODERN ROMANCE:

PART 2

Maggie loved riddles! Glenn couldn't figure out why she liked them so much – maybe they appealed to her analytical mind – but she clearly couldn't get enough of solving them.

Having exhausted the patience of the farm's other residents, Glenn paid a visit to the local library while on a supply run. It had largely escaped the scavenging that depleted the town's other buildings, yet he couldn't find a single volume to assist him. The detour prompted a thought, however, and when he returned he asked Maggie the following:

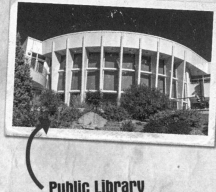

Public Library

Q "Why is a Duke like a book?"

24 UNSAFE SAFE CRACKING

Although Georgia had lately become home to many terrors, Rickard Safes were always a welcome sight. It was plainly apparent that the company would have gone swiftly out of business if the world hadn't beaten it to the punch: while the strongboxes were as physically impregnable as their TV commercials boasted, their override codes could be deduced by solving a puzzle on the keypad. As long as you could unlock one before a walker attacked, you'd usually be rewarded with a weapon or two, alongside several useless stacks of money.

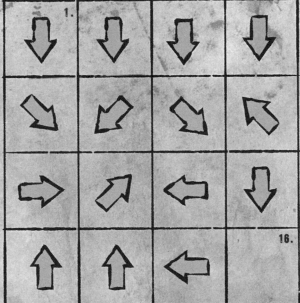

To unlock the safe, move from top left to bottom right, stopping on each square exactly once. The arrows in each square show which direction you must move in.

Solution on page 176

39

Lurkers

25 THE LAST FARM:

PART 1

To the best of Hershel's knowledge, there wasn't a single other establishment still functioning in the county. The high school was abandoned. The hospital had burned down. The main street was closed for business. All that was left was his family's farm, miraculously untouched. If the farm hadn't stopped, he couldn't either: the fields still needed tilling and the animals still needed tending.

To cope with the sudden influx of new people, he'd planted another crop of vegetables for the autumn; thinking so far ahead was a luxury that most couldn't afford any more, but he couldn't afford not to.

Hershel's new garden was ten rods' square and required fencing to protect it from wildlife. The fence posts were placed exactly one rod apart,

Q So how many posts did he need to use?

Lurkers 40 Solution on page 176

PART 2

Nobody had bothered to inform the cows that they were living through the end times. Hershel's black and brown bovine continued to eat, sleep and laze about like everything was completely normal.

Fortunately, this had meant a steady supply of milk and other dairy for the farm's existing occupants but, with the addition of Rick and his group, Hershel needed to decide which type of cow he should focus on breeding. He found that four brown and three black cows gave as much milk in five days as three brown and five black ones gave in four days.

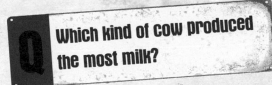

Q Which kind of cow produced the most milk?

27 THE LAST FARM:

PART 3

One of the benefits of hosting so many new people was that there were more hands to help out with the labour. This was valuable, given Hershel's advancing years and the general uselessness of Beth's boyfriend, Jimmy.

Hershel had calculated that five people could pack five crates of apples in five minutes.

Q How many people would be required to pack 50 crates in 50 minutes?

Lurkers

42

Solution on page 177

2|8 BAD COP

Shane's "interrogation" of his captive was not going well. For some reason, Randall seemed more concerned with the pain that was being doled out to him than answering the officer's questions. He refused to state where his group was camped, or even how many of them there were.

The only real information that Shane could beat out of him was that all but two of the men were from Augusta, all but two of the men were born in Columbus, and all but two of the men were originally from Macon. There was also a woman from Valdosta. After he was done, Shane gruffly relayed the information to Rick, who immediately knew exactly how many people they needed to worry about.

Q How many were in the group?

Solution on page 177

43

Lurkers

There are 10 differences between the picture on the left and the image on the right. Can you spot them?

Lurkers

44

30 COUNTING THE DEAD

That man was more dangerous than any walker, Hershel thought as Shane smashed the doors of the barn. He was yelling that times had changed, and he was right about that: for Hershel, this was truly the end of the way things had been. As much as he'd ever believed in anything – God, his family, the bottle – he'd maintained that the epidemic would pass, that there would be a way to cure his friends and loved ones inside the barn.

Now it didn't matter. The dead stumbled out into the daylight to meet their fate. In his mind, Hershel transformed the walkers into numbers to block out the pain. A fifth had come from his own family. A third were neighbours from the next farm over. Three times the difference between those two numbers had been friends from his church. He knew them all; had loved them all.

Lurkers

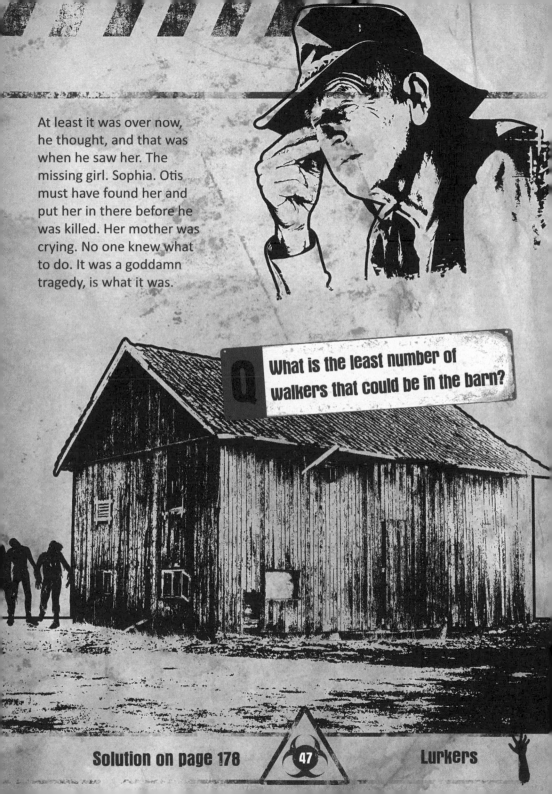

At least it was over now, he thought, and that was when he saw her. The missing girl. Sophia. Otis must have found her and put her in there before he was killed. Her mother was crying. No one knew what to do. It was a goddamn tragedy, is what it was.

Q What is the least number of walkers that could be in the barn?

Solution on page 178

Lurkers

SEASON 3

BITERS

PART 1

They'd exhausted their best stories by the end of the first month, their worst ones by the end of the second. As prisoners, they were more accustomed to the experience of isolation than most, but ten months inside a cafeteria would be a maddening challenge for anyone. After the riot and the bloodshed and the dead bodies coming back to life, the five men were grateful to not be in active danger any more, but remained stranded without anything to do except wait for a rescue that wouldn't come.

Andrew and Tomas mostly sulked and kept to themselves but the other three made elaborate efforts to entertain the others. While charades and re-enacting half-remembered television episodes got old quickly, one surprisingly durable pursuit was dumbfounding their fellow inmates with riddles. They could spend days at a time just trying to think of the perfect problem, taking pride in being able to outsmart one another. The endeavour had been initiated by Big Tiny, who had approached the others one day, absolutely beaming, and said,

"What always runs and never walks, often murmurs, never talks, What has a bed but never sleeps, what has a mouth but never eats?"

PART 2

Oscar had been the one to crack Big Tiny's riddle, causing Axel to brood for a full hour before gracefully conceding defeat.

The trio decided that Oscar's victory meant it was his turn to go next. He took this responsibility seriously and spent an afternoon combing the cafeteria for inspiration. Nothing came to mind, so they continued with their usual itinerary of card games and describing implausible erotic encounters they'd claimed to have experienced. That night, however, he woke the others as they slept and yelled into their faces,

"You use a knife to slice my head, then weep beside me when I'm dead."

Q What was the answer to Oscar's riddle?

Solution on page 179

51

BITERS

PART 3

Axel couldn't solve this riddle either, and he wondered if his failure to do so explained something about why he ended up in prison for conducting armed robbery with a water pistol.

It was evident that Big Tiny had something in mind – over the following months, they would discover that he always had a riddle ready to go – because no sooner had he answered Oscar's problem than he gave his own:

"One hundred and fifty, when joined to a tree, makes a fine garment that warms you and me."

PART 4

Solving Big Tiny's riddle before Oscar was possibly Axel's proudest ever moment, although that said more about his own life up until that point than about the value of the achievement itself.

Regardless, he wholly intended to milk the moment for all it was worth — something which lead to Tomas threatening his life on more than one occasion. The risk of violent death was worth it, if only for Oscar's mild embarrassment. He ultimately appreciated the intimidating behaviour anyway, as it inspired a riddle that would nearly displace his earlier personal apogee:

"What's the difference between a cloud and a beaten prisoner?"

What is Rick Grimes doing below?

Column clues (top, left to right):
| | | | | | | | | | | | | | 4 | | | | | 4 | 7 2 2 | | |
|1|1|1|2|3|2|1|2|2|3|3|3|3|4 1|17|22|23|23|17|16|2|6|6|

Row clues (top to bottom):
2
4
4
4
5 4
3 3
8 6
13
12
9
7
7
8
8
8
6 1
6 1
6 2
7 1
7 1
6 1
7 1
8 1

To reveal the image, shade the grid's cells so that each column and row has continuous shaded blocks of the lengths indicated by the numbers at the start of that column or row, with at least one empty cell between each block.

BITERS

54

Solution on page 180

36 A DEATH SENTENCE

"Woodbury has gone to hell."

The Governor regarded Milton with his one good eye.

"I don't think Woodbury is alone in that distinction, do you?"

Milton had fetched him to solve a dispute: a man lay in the centre of the main street, knifed to death. The Governor asked what had happened.

"It was Paul," Shumpert said,

Paul's eyes widened. "He's lying!"

"Shumpert did it," Crowley offered.

"Well, it wasn't me," said Josh.

Milton looked from man to man, then back to The Governor.

"I don't know how I know, but I'm certain three of them are lying."

The Governor nodded. He pulled his gun from its holster and shot the guilty man dead. "We don't kill in Woodbury," he said.

Q **Who did The Governor shoot?**

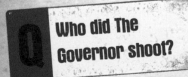

Solution on page 181

55

BITERS

Carol probably thought about chocolate every single day. It was impossible to have made it this far and not lost people – in fact, to have lost almost everyone you'd ever known – but it was the absence of the little things that acted as a constant reminder that your previous life had disappeared entirely.

Given Carol's brute of a dead husband, this wasn't all bad, but still: she missed chocolate like it was a person. Tragically, she'd rarely even bought it before the outbreak, afraid to treat herself – although Ed said that chocolate was better than nothing, he preferred pretzels, and so pretzels was what she bought.

To the great surprise of both parties involved, chocolate was at the heart of one of the only fights she ever had with Lori. She had announced, in atypically grandiose fashion, that chocolate was better than eternal happiness, and Lori, while an appreciator of chocolate in all of its form, wouldn't go quite that far. Nothing was better than eternal happiness, she stated, and the two argued for some time before they came to the only logical conclusion.

Q What was better: chocolate or eternal happiness?

38 MISSING THE TRAIN

"**DUANE TURNED**" screamed the wall in thick blood letters. Morgan's home had become a headache of weaponry and troubling graffiti, the contents of a disturbed psyche splashed across every available surface. As Morgan lay unconscious on the cot bed, Rick contemplated the mind of his friend – the man who'd saved his life, taken care of him, set him on his way. How had he fallen so far, and was there a way back?

Rick could barely read what was on the walls, let alone understand their meaning. Just about the only thing he could figure out – in terms of its answer, anyway – was an odd question about distances, written above a map:

"A train leaves from King County to Atlanta and, half an hour later, a train leaves at the same speed from Atlanta to King County. Which is nearer to Atlanta when they meet?"

57 **BITERS**

Rickard safes were designed for the connoisseur scavenger. As would have become embarrassingly evident to the creators if they hadn't all died, the safe override codes could be easily found by solving a puzzle on their keypads. This action would provide their looter with a handgun at the minimum, and usually enough cash/kindling to start a small fire.

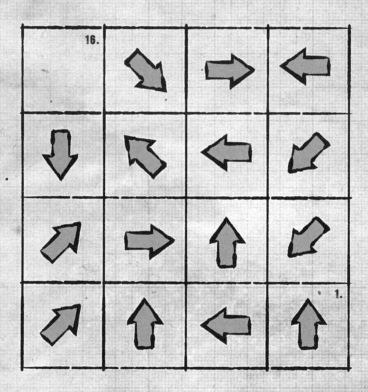

To unlock the safe, move from bottom right to top left, stopping on each square exactly once. The arrows in each square show which direction you must move in.

BITERS

Solution on page 182

40 THE QUIZZING DEAD

1. WHO IS THE FIRST CHARACTER IN THE SERIES TO BE BITTEN BY A WALKER AND SURVIVE?

2. WHY DOES CAROL ASK GLENN TO HELP HER CATCH A WALKER?

3. WHAT DOES THE GOVERNOR KEEP IN HIS PRIVATE ROOM?

4. WHY DOES CARL VISIT KING COUNTY CAFE?

5. WHAT IS THE GOVERNOR'S REAL NAME?

6. WHEN THE GROUP RESCUE MAGGIE AND GLENN FROM WOODBURY, WHO DOES RICK HALLUCINATE SEEING?

7. WHY DOES THE GOVERNOR NEED AN EYE PATCH?

8. WHAT IS DARYL'S NICKNAME FOR JUDITH GRIMES?

9. WHAT ENTERTAINMENT DOES THE GOVERNOR PUT ON FOR THE PEOPLE OF WOODBURY?

10. WHO BURNS THE PIT WALKERS?

SEASON 3 HARD

1. WHAT JOB DID ANDREA HAVE BEFORE THE WALKER OUTBREAK?

2. MERLE DIXON RETURNS IN SEASON 3, HAVING AMPUTATED HIMSELF TO ESCAPE A DEPARTMENT-STORE ROOF. WHICH BODY PART IS HE MISSING?

3. AT HERSHEL'S REQUEST, WHAT DRINKING SONG DO MAGGIE AND BETH SING AT THE CAMPFIRE?

4. HOW LONG WERE THE FIVE PRISONERS TRAPPED IN THE CAFETERIA?

5. HOW DID THE GOVERNOR'S WIFE DIE?

6. WHAT TERM DO THE RESIDENTS OF WOODBURY USE TO DESCRIBE THE UNDEAD?

WOODBERRY

7. WHAT'S THE NAME OF THE 14-YEAR-OLD ASTHMATIC THAT THE GOVERNOR ENLISTS IN HIS ARMY?

8. WHAT PART OF THE PRISON DO THE GROUP USE AS A BASE?

9. WHAT SONG DOES MILTON PLAY TO MR COLEMAN WHEN RESEARCHING TRACE MEMORY IN WALKERS?

10. HOW DOES GLENN GET AN ENGAGEMENT RING FOR MAGGIE?

42 "THE FESTIVITIES":

PART 1

"Just because the world has ended doesn't mean we can't have a little fun."

Merle turned to Michonne and flashed what could only be described as a smile in the strictest technical sense of the term.

"Give it back. Let me leave."

"Come and have a look at something first. Come on."

They joined a crowd gathered on what had once been high-school bleachers in another life. As the amassed spectators hurled rocks and obscenities, a family of walkers shambled around a makeshift course, numbers painted on their backs. To deafening, ecstatic cheers, Martinez sliced off one of the leading walker's legs with Michonne's katana.

It was a cold world, and Michonne had endured more than her fair share of it, but this was something else. The only word she could think of was monstrous.

"Figure this out, darling, and you can have your toy." He smiled his non-smile. **"If that biter overtakes the one in second place, what position will it be in?"**

61

BITERS

PART 2

Merle shrugged at the correct answer, and Michonne understood that she was dealing with a man who played dirty pool. **"Whatever. If you're not a fan of athletics, we have fights too. I always win."**

"Is that a fact?" she asked. Merle's lips curled at the corners of his mouth. He called to Milton, who squeezed past half a row of knees and their annoyed owners.

"Ask our sweetheart a question about 'Little' and 'Large' over there." Merle gestured towards the track with his stump. **"Something real tough, though."**

With the clipped swiftness of a man eager to return to being miserable somewhere else, Milton said the following:

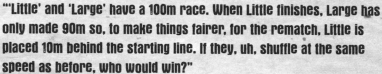

"'Little' and 'Large' have a 100m race. When Little finishes, Large has only made 90m so, to make things fairer, for the rematch, Little is placed 10m behind the starting line. If they, uh, shuffle at the same speed as before, who would win?"

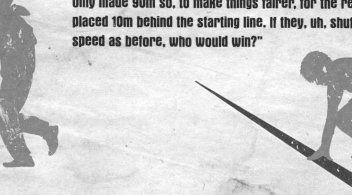

BITERS

62

Solution on page 184

PART 3

Merle tensed his remaining fist in a way that suggested he wished he'd brought along his hand-blade. "Again, Miltie. Ask her something that's actually difficult."

"With all due respect, did you know the answer?"

"Of course he did!" Michonne jumped in. "I bet he could get the next one too and, if he doesn't, I'm allowed to leave and that idiot down there will stop ruining my sword."

Milton knew better than to smile. On the track there were only two walkers remaining, although that was no longer a fitting description, given that one was missing its bottom half entirely.

"Presuming that your man doesn't deprive anyone else of any further limbs, Large can complete a lap in six minutes, while it takes Little just four to do the same. If they both start from the same point, how many minutes before Little laps Large?"

Instead of the impressively wrong answer he gave, what should Merle have said to have stopped Michonne leaving?

45 ALARMED

Noise was death. If a walker could hear you, it could find you. That was why the sudden activation of the prison's alarm system left the group in catastrophic danger, and also why Rick was so keen to enter the tombs to disable the back-up generator, even if it meant a run-in with whomever switched it on.

Start

Q Help Rick find the generator.

Given the present circumstances, the idea of a bad day had mostly lost its meaning but, if they still existed, Daryl was certainly having one.

From the guard tower, Carol watched him approach the gates of the prison. He had exchanged his crossbow for a limp and a foul mood.

"Heavens, what happened to you? You've been gone eight hours. Where's your bike?"

"I'd finally found a pharmacy when someone jumped me, didn't they."

"Well, there's no use pouting. You can track. Let's go and get it. How far away was the place?"

Factoring in the blocked roads and walker-clearing, he'd been riding at a speed of only 9mph. After he'd lost his bike, he guessed that he'd been even slower returning, walking at 3mph. Maybe it was the blow to the head but Daryl was stumped. Carol, though, quickly figured out the answer to her own question.

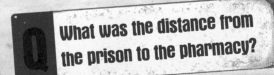

Q What was the distance from the prison to the pharmacy?

47 NEW FRIENDS

The Governor's interpretation of keeping Woodbury safe was to eliminate anyone he thought remotely posed a threat. This constituted, it was fair to say, almost everyone he encountered.

A prime example: on a sticky summer day, Woodbury was visited by a trio of army reservists who had been on a training exercise during the initial outbreak. The three young men were the only surviving members of their unit but, aside from malnourishment, they were healthy and eager to contribute.

Greeting them cheerfully, The Governor invited the soldiers to his private garden to enjoy a pitcher of some cold, refreshing lemonade. As the men politely sipped their drinks, The Governor downed his thirstily, citing the warmth of the afternoon. He listened to their story with care and attention, and told them they'd be welcome to join the town once they'd retrieved their belongings from their camp. Strangely, though, the men never returned to Woodbury, and The Governor never set eyes (or just one eye) on them again. **"They must have fallen victim to a couple of biters,"** The Governor later remarked.

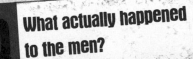

Q What actually happened to the men?

The prison had been compromised. From the guard tower, Glenn watched in horror as walkers swarmed the yard. His friends' only hope was that he was a good shot.

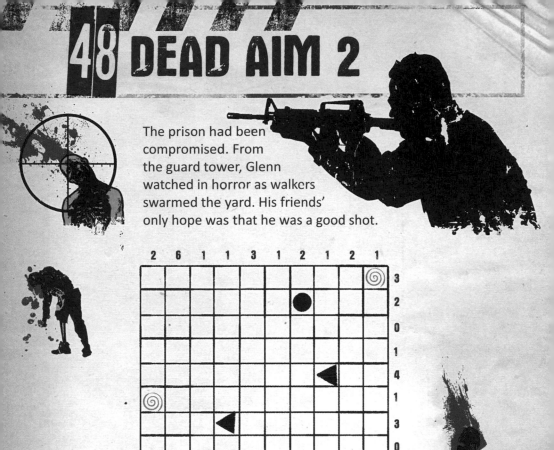

	2	6	1	1	3	1	2	1	2	1	
											3
											2
											0
											1
											4
											1
											3
											0
											3
											3

HUMANS   **CARS**   **GROUPS OF WALKERS**

INDIVIDUAL WALKERS   **WALKER HERD**

Identify the exact locations of the walkers and humans hidden in this image. All are positioned horizontally or vertically and no one is immediately adjacent to anyone else, including diagonally. The row and column numbers indicate the total segments in their corresponding lines.

PART 1

Maggie and Glenn had been together for nearly a year and she still couldn't bear to tell him that she didn't love riddles. She enjoyed them well enough, of course, but, when she'd fallen for a sweet ex-pizza delivery boy, she hadn't expected to be receiving them as gifts once a week for the rest of her life. The lengths he went to in pursuit of new riddles was touching, undoubtedly, but it would have been nice to spend just a little less time being utterly confounded.

She was reminded of all this when she returned from a long night shift at the guard tower to find yet another slip of paper waiting on her pillow. By that point she was tired enough to sleep for several weeks, but the riddle was having none of it: Maggie knew, maddeningly, that she would be unable to rest until she'd worked it out. The slip of paper said,

"If from your shelf you take a book,
You'll find me there if you but look;
And if you put me back again,
That I am there is also plain;
Decapitate, it will then appear
Without mistake that I am here;
Behead again — you'll want no more,
Because I always come before."

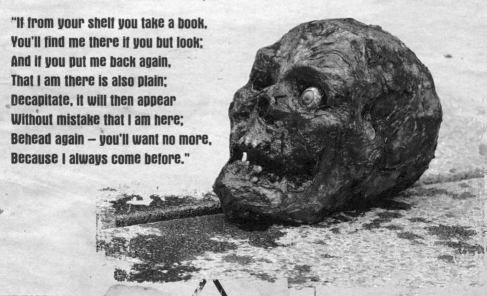

BITERS

68

Solution on page 188

50 PILLOW PROBLEMS:

PART 2

Their first anniversary was approaching – or at least Glenn assumed it was approaching... he'd sort of lost track of the months – and he wanted to do something special for Maggie. He was planning to ask her to marry him but he felt that a truly excellent riddle would be the icing on the cake. Or maybe he could find a way to make a cake? No, that was ridiculous: she would much prefer a riddle, obviously.

Glenn discarded a score of potential riddles as unworthy of the occasion. He was looking for a riddle harder than any he'd asked before. Failing in that task, he decided that quantity was better than quality, and quickly left three riddles on her pillow:

"What is bought by the yard and worn by the foot?"

"Why does a sick person lose their sense of touch?"

"What's always coming but never arrives?"

Solution on page 188

69

BITERS

51 THE GRAVEYARD SHIFT

As the world fell to bits, one of the first things to vanish was the concept of a good night's sleep. How could anyone sleep properly when something as minor as a quick nap might result in death? Even if a companion had agreed to watch over you, there was no guarantee that they wouldn't be suddenly overwhelmed by walkers, or nod off themselves in the boredom of the night. It wasn't worth the risk.

The prison, by contrast, was an idyll: all those fences, all those gates, all those walls. Such security required constant vigilance to maintain, but that felt like a small price. The prison council agreed that the four appointed guards would each work a pair of six-hour shifts a day, with a break in between. These shifts would start precisely on the hour so that there were always two people on duty – one in the tower, one killing walkers at the fence – and as such, no one changed shifts at the same time.

Due to the crucial and demanding nature of the role, the council attempted to be as accommodating as possible. Sasha – an early riser – wanted to be on duty at 9 am. Maggie was appalled by the very thought, and asked if she could start at midnight and be finished by 4 pm. Carol needed to be free to "read books" to the children between 10 am and 4 pm, and Glenn agreed to relieve her after his second shift.

Q What hours did everyone guard the prison?

SKIN EATERS

Solution on page 168

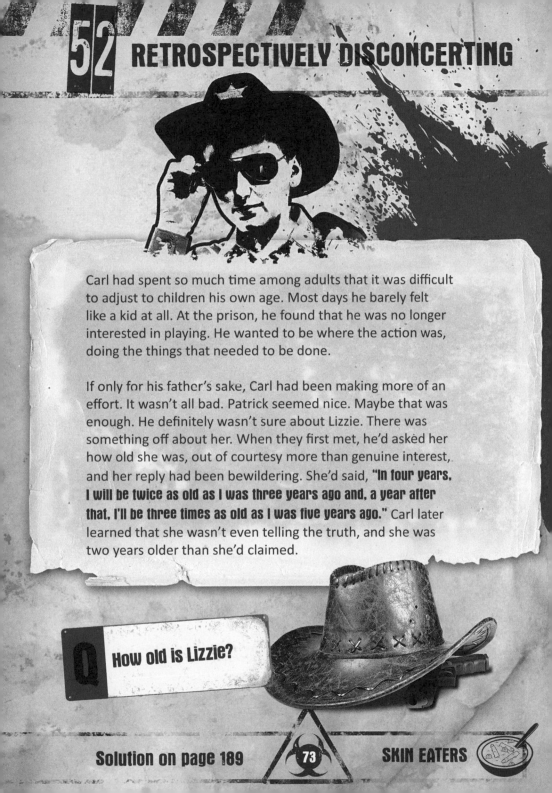

Carl had spent so much time among adults that it was difficult to adjust to children his own age. Most days he barely felt like a kid at all. At the prison, he found that he was no longer interested in playing. He wanted to be where the action was, doing the things that needed to be done.

If only for his father's sake, Carl had been making more of an effort. It wasn't all bad. Patrick seemed nice. Maybe that was enough. He definitely wasn't sure about Lizzie. There was something off about her. When they first met, he'd asked her how old she was, out of courtesy more than genuine interest, and her reply had been bewildering. She'd said, **"In four years, I will be twice as old as I was three years ago and, a year after that, I'll be three times as old as I was five years ago."** Carl later learned that she wasn't even telling the truth, and she was two years older than she'd claimed.

Q How old is Lizzie?

53 SPOT THE DIFFERENCE 2

There are 10 differences between the picture on the left and the image on the right. Can you spot them?

 **SKIN EATERS**

 74

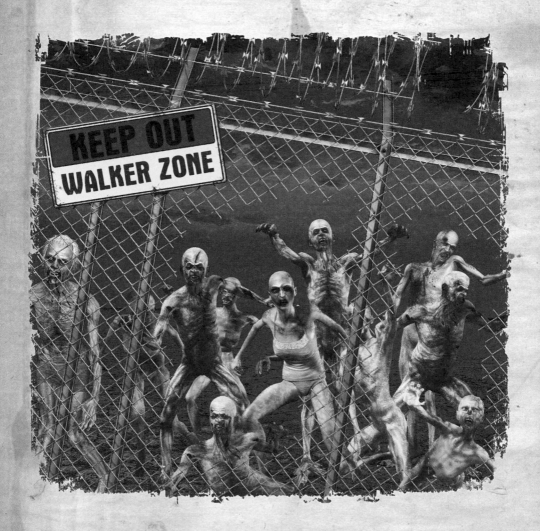

"How many walkers have you killed?"

People would say almost anything to receive sanctuary at the prison. The meanest crook was suddenly a saint and, if you took them at their word, who knows what trouble would ensue. The prison council decided that the most sensible approach was to ask all prospective guests the same three questions. It wasn't foolproof but gave a fair indication of what skills someone possessed, what they had been through and, most importantly, what they were willing to do to survive.

On a supply run to look for car parts, Rick found a pair of women holed up in a tyre warehouse. In answer to Rick's first question, both women claimed that they'd killed several dozen walkers, and then the first woman said, **"You don't believe us? Either I'm a liar or she was telling the truth."**

Q What conclusion did Rick come to?

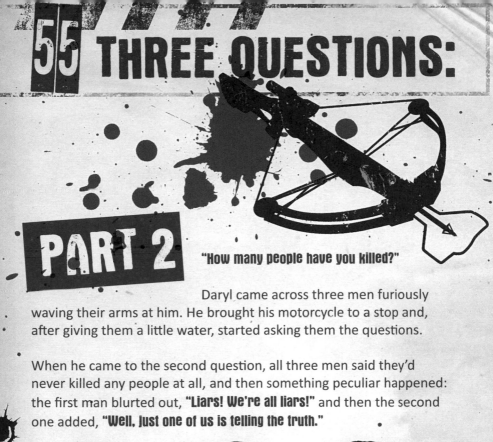

PART 2

"How many people have you killed?"

Daryl came across three men furiously waving their arms at him. He brought his motorcycle to a stop and, after giving them a little water, started asking them the questions.

When he came to the second question, all three men said they'd never killed any people at all, and then something peculiar happened: the first man blurted out, **"Liars! We're all liars!"** and then the second one added, **"Well, just one of us is telling the truth."**

Q Did Daryl rescue any of the men?

Solution on page 190
77
SKIN EATERS

56 THREE QUESTIONS:

PART 3

"Why?"

Michonne met the most confusing group of all, which was unfortunate as she also had the least patience for tomfoolery. She ran into three people: Amanda, Lauren and Edwin – she was the only person to bother to actually ask their names – who were ransacking a pet-food shop, rather desperately. All of them claimed to have killed people only in self-defence. Amanda said that Lauren was lying, while Lauren said that Amanda and Edwin were either both lying or both telling the truth.

Q Was Edwin worth taking back to the prison?

 SKIN EATERS

 78

Solution on page 191

What brutal weapon is concealed below?

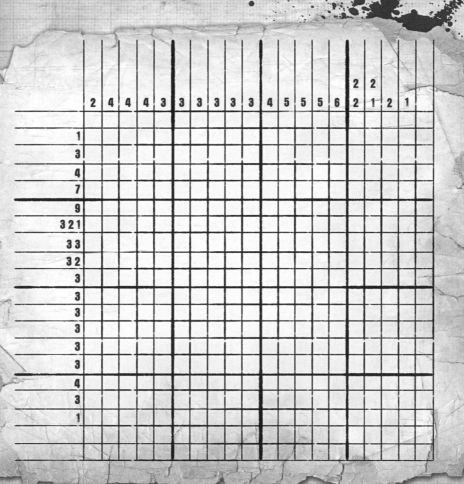

To reveal the image, shade the grid's cells so that each column and row has continuous shaded blocks of the lengths indicated by the numbers at the start of that column or row, with at least one empty cell between each block.

79

SKIN EATERS

For the first time in his life, Daryl was respected. It seemed like every time he went on another run, he found a new group of strangers to bring back to the prison, and they showered him with appreciation. This made him a little uncomfortable but it wasn't the worst feeling in the world; more than the gratitude itself, he liked the idea of being a person worthy of such strong feelings. Not that he would ever mention this out loud, of course.

Daryl wasn't the only one who had been wrangling survivors. Michonne had rescued more people than Rick, while Bob and Daryl between themselves had saved as many people as Rick and Michonne, and Bob and Michonne hadn't rescued as many as Daryl and Rick.

Q Who had brought the most, second most, third most and least number of people to the prison?

SKIN EATERS

Solution on page 193

Life was too short to have regrets, and getting shorter all the time. Despite this, the fine people at the Rickard Safes and Vaults Company, USA, would have probably spared the time to regret their easily cracked safes if their headquarters hadn't been swamped by walkers on the first day of the outbreak. It was discovered – not by them but by many grateful plunderers – that each safe's override codes could be deduced by solving a puzzle on its security keypad: a design flaw that reliably provided Georgia's dwindling non-dead population with racy magazines and much-needed weaponry.

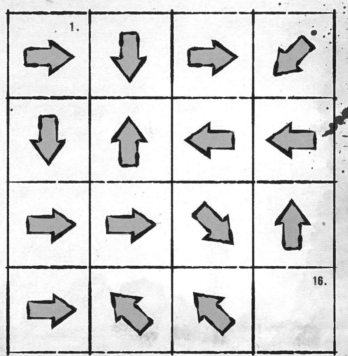

To unlock the safe, move from top left to bottom right, stopping on each square exactly once. The arrows in each square show which direction you must move in.

81

SKIN EATERS

60 THE QUIZZING DEAD

1. ACCORDING TO BETH'S SIGN, HOW MANY DAYS HAS IT BEEN WITHOUT AN ACCIDENT AT THE PRISON?

2. WHAT LESSON DOES CAROL GIVE TO THE PRISON'S CHILDREN INSTEAD OF READING THEM A BOOK?

3. WHAT IS DR CALEB SUBRAMANIAN BETTER KNOWN AS?

4. WHAT ITEM DOES BOB SCAVENGE AT THE VETERINARY COLLEGE INSTEAD OF MEDICINE?

5. WHO WAS FEEDING RATS TO WALKERS AT THE PRISON FENCE?

6. WHAT DOES RICK FIND BURIED IN HIS GARDEN?

7. WHAT IS THE CONNECTION BETWEEN MICHONNE AND HER TWO WALKER BODYGUARDS?

8. WHO ARE THE MEMBERS OF THE PRISON COUNCIL?

9. WHERE DOES EUGENE SAY HE WORKS?

10. WHO DOES THE GOVERNOR DECAPITATE WITH MICHONNE'S KATANA?

1. WHO IS THE FIRST VICTIM OF THE PRISON INFECTION?

2. WHAT DOES LILLY ASK THE GOVERNOR TO RETRIEVE AT A NEARBY NURSING HOME?

3. WHEN HIS FATHER GETS INJURED, CARL SITS ON THE ROOF OF A HOUSE AND EATS WHAT?

4. WHAT DOES ZACH GUESS WAS DARYL'S PROFESSION BEFORE THE TURN?

SEASON 4 HARD

5. CAROL, TYREESE, LIZZIE AND MIKA TAKE REFUGE AT A HOUSE THAT'S IN THE MIDDLE OF WHAT?

6. WHAT FAKE NAME DOES THE GOVERNOR GIVE TO TARA AND LILLY?

7. WHEN BETH AND DARYL RAID A COUNTRY CLUB, BETH DECIDES SHE WANTS TO HAVE HER FIRST ALCOHOLIC DRINK. WHAT DRINK DOES DARYL REFUSE TO LET HER HAVE?

8. WHAT DOES MIKA CALL THE RAGDOLL SHE FINDS?

9. WHO DOES CAROL KILL IN AN ATTEMPT TO STOP THE INFECTION SPREADING AT THE PRISON?

10. WHAT IS DARYL ACCUSED OF STEALING BY LEN?

Solution on page 194

83

SKIN EATERS

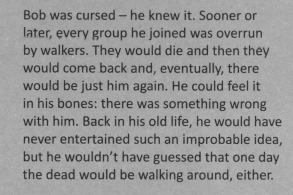

Bob was cursed — he knew it. Sooner or later, every group he joined was overrun by walkers. They would die and then they would come back and, eventually, there would be just him again. He could feel it in his bones: there was something wrong with him. Back in his old life, he would have never entertained such an improbable idea, but he wouldn't have guessed that one day the dead would be walking around, either.

The first time it happened was shortly after it all started. Bob had been taken in by two mothers and two daughters. Each carried a rifle — not that it did them any good. He returned from scavenging to find that they'd turned and were now lumbering around in the basement. After burying the bodies, he took their three guns and went out into the night. He needed a drink.

Q How can this be?

SKIN EATERS

84

Solution on page 195

As the National Guard was stubbornly refusing to show up, and their only company beyond each other was a seven-year-old girl and a dying man, Tara and Lilly had a lot of time on their hands. The pair were both keen readers but, over the year, they'd managed to read every book in the apartment multiple times – even the terrible ones. If matters persisted any longer, they would be able to recite the assorted tomes from memory, which would at least kill a few more hours.

Once or twice, they attempted to play a card game against each other but neither had the temperament for the activity. Tara suggested making it more interesting – almost any addition would accomplish this, they felt – by playing for a stake of one cent each hand. Unsurprisingly, this also failed to do the trick: by the time they gave up for good, Lilly had won three hands and Tara had three cents.

Q How many hands did Tara and Lilly play?

Tyreese didn't know why but he had always been good with children. They saw him as a bit of a pushover, he suspected, which was impressive considering that he used to be an NFL linebacker.

From early on he felt instinctively protective over both Lizzie and Mika. It was like there was some dark thing following them that he could feel but not see. Lizzie, undoubtedly, had her problems but there was a sadness to Mika too. He would come up with little problems to entertain her, although she usually figured them out before he could even finish his thought. The one he was most proud of, and that took her about a minute to crack, was the following:

"A Jacksonville truck driver was heading down Union Street – a while ago, of course. The man is exhausted – so exhausted, in fact, that he ignores every single stop sign. He mounts the sidewalk as a cop car passes, then travels the wrong way down a one-way street. So why didn't anyone arrest him? Tell me that!"

SKIN EATERS

65 END OF THE LINE

Getting to Terminus wasn't complicated. You just had to follow the train tracks, stay vigilant for threats and feel a spark of hope every time you saw one of the signs. But what should you do when you've been run off the path by a herd of walkers, with no clear idea about how to find it again?

Start

Sasha was presently in this very situation; something not helped by the thought that her companions had probably already arrived — maybe they were even enjoying a proper meal at last.

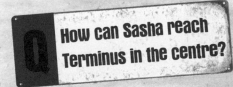

How can Sasha reach Terminus in the centre?

 87

SKIN EATERS

SEASON 5

ROAMERS

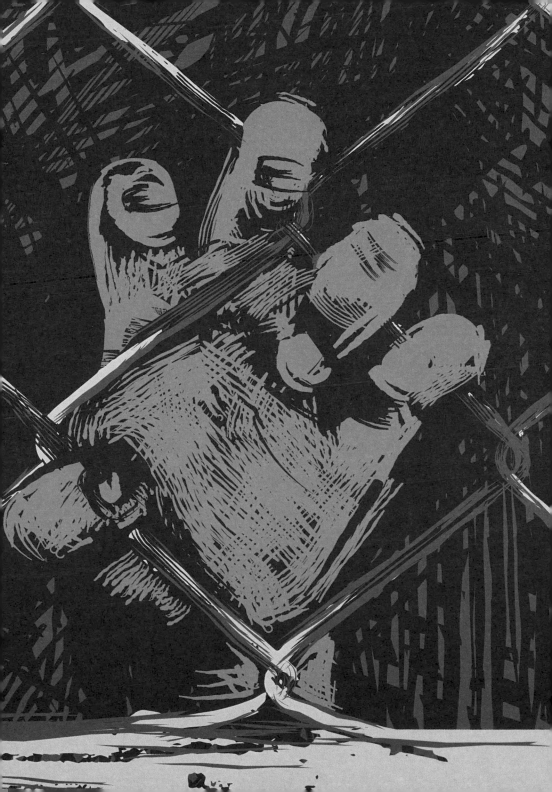

Eugene squinted in the direction of his friend and shook his head.

"With all due respect you're wholly wrong. In this man's opinion — I would not classify it as humble, but that is neither here nor there — the bridge is indeed crossable, it just happens to demand adherence to certain conditions. The accelerating deterioration of infrastructure in this region being what it is, the bridge can only hold two people at a time, and our single military-grade flashlight must be used throughout each crossing to avoid us tumbling into the ravine below. Incidentally, this also means that any crossing must be undertaken at the pace of the slowest person, which is regrettable given that the throng of dead ones are fifteen minutes away from our position.

I estimate that Abraham, as the most robust member of our group, could cross the bridge in one minute flat, Rosita in two minutes, Rex in five minutes and myself, as a self-confessed coward who is fearful of blunt trauma caused by falling from a rickety bridge, could cross in eight minutes. This puts us under considerable strain, I admit, but I do believe that we can all get across safely before we are overwhelmed by the superior numbers and baneful disposition of our undead antagonists. Trust me, I'm smarter than you".

Q Is Eugene right?

ROAMERS

PART 1

Glenn wasn't sure if he'd ever been so glad to see five words before. The first sign said "GLENN GO TO TERMINUS MAGGIE", and the second one, too. As the group marched along the railroad tracks he watched Sasha and Bob's names join his wife's, and he thought that would be the end of it, until the glorious moment when he spied a sheet of defaced corrugated iron that read:

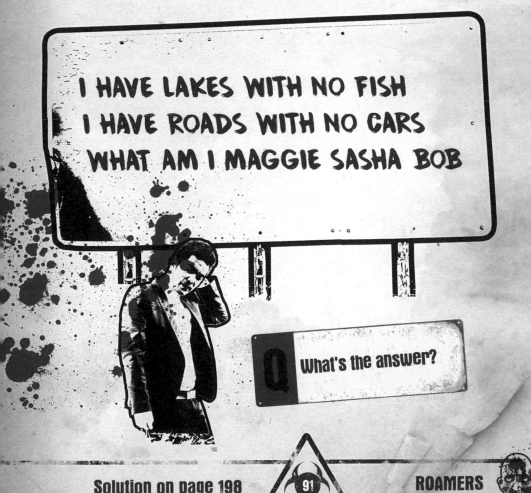

I HAVE LAKES WITH NO FISH
I HAVE ROADS WITH NO CARS
WHAT AM I MAGGIE SASHA BOB

Q what's the answer?

Solution on page 198

91

ROAMERS

68 A WAYS AWAY:

PART 2

The paint was dry, the dispatched walkers had long since caught the attention of indiscriminate crows and coyotes, but every time Glenn spotted one of Maggie's riddles it was as if he would find her around the next corner. Literally and figuratively, they were signs – a smile and a wave, meant only for him. He felt a strange sort of pride as each one appeared down the road, although he also couldn't help blushing when he saw the following:

WHAT HAS FEET AND LEGS
BUT NOTHING ELSE MAGGIE
BOB SASHA

Q What's the answer?

ROAMERS

92

Solution on page 198

PART 3

There isn't always a lot of room for surprise in a marriage, especially one where you're compelled by apocalyptic circumstances to spend almost all of your time together.

Despite their imposed, extended intimacy, Glenn was delighted and surprised to find that Maggie's wit was present even in her riddles. He'd never even contemplated that she might approach them in a different way, but when he saw the following painted onto a railway sleeper he understood both that they were getting close and that his wife was making fun of him.

WHEN IS A CANDLE LIKE A TOMBSTONE MAGGIE SASHA BOB

Q What's the answer?

It would be nice, Sasha thought, if she could wake up one day and not have anything attempt to eat her. Things were getting ridiculous: if it wasn't the walkers it was the cannibals, and just how tasty was human flesh anyway? Couldn't these people learn to love salads? How hard was it to make a sandwich?

These thoughts distracted her from the trouble she was in: the distinctly uncool people of Terminus had revealed their intention to eat all of the group, and their reasons for this were unconvincing at best. Sasha had been nominally designated as the first course, but Gareth made her a perverse offer:

"If you make a statement that's true we will broil you over a fire, and if you make a statement that's false we will boil you in a pot."

Q What did Sasha say to spare her life?

Tyreese had been through worse scrapes than this, although no examples came to mind. As he awaited death at the hands – and mouths – of Terminus' cannibal crew, he scanned the room for some means of escape.

The results weren't promising: the walls were stone, the only light came from a window too high to reach, and although the ground was made of earth, it would take a lifetime to tunnel out. Even the door, locked from the outside, was a thick, hostile slab of metal. At least they seemed to be experienced in their depraved practices, he thought, so maybe being dinner would be as relatively painless as such a thing can be.

Just as Tyreese was wondering whether it would be worse to be eaten by a walker or a human, he grinned, understanding exactly what he needed to do.

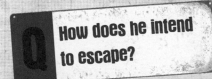

Q How does he intend to escape?

72 UNSAFE SAFE CRACKING 4

Before they were assailed by a horde of walkers, the makers of Rickard Safes were presumably very nice people just trying to live their lives. Yes, their safes could be easily unlocked by solving a puzzle on the keypad, but other than that the objects were impregnable. Nobody's perfect. Fortunately, this grievous flaw provided countless scavengers with weapons, which might have comforted the designers if their reanimated bodies weren't now lurching around the company's break room.

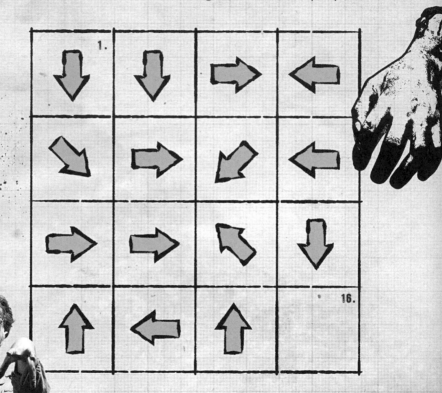

To unlock the safe, move from top left to bottom right, stopping on each square exactly once. The arrows in each square show which direction you must move in.

ROAMERS 96 **Solution on page 199**

PART 1

Rosita knew it wasn't geographically feasible but some days it felt like Washington was getting further away instead of closer. She believed in their mission to deliver Eugene to D.C. – as Abraham said, it might fix the whole damn world – but they were hard miles, especially with the loss of Stephanie, Rex, Pam and the others.

Cooped up together in the truck's cabin, Eugene took it upon himself to lighten the mood, which usually prompted bemusement rather than other reactions. As they left the ruins of Houston behind, he declared:

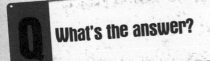

"Despite my idiosyncratic demeanour I am not an only child: my sister is two years older than me and my brother was born four years before she was. My mother, who is gone now, rest her soul, was 28 when I was born, and the average age of all of us would be 39... if we were all still breathing, that is. So what is my age?"

Q What's the answer?

PART 2

They tried to avoid the major conurbations but sometimes the country roads would be so deadly and vehicle-choked that their only hope was to take their chances in the city. As they drove through Lake Charles with their windows rolled up, Eugene turned to his companions and said:

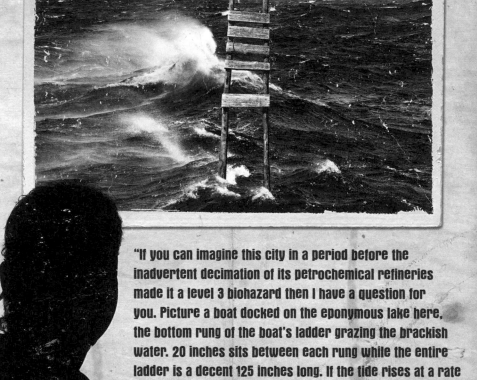

"If you can imagine this city in a period before the inadvertent decimation of its petrochemical refineries made it a level 3 biohazard then I have a question for you. Picture a boat docked on the eponymous lake here, the bottom rung of the boat's ladder grazing the brackish water. 20 inches sits between each rung while the entire ladder is a decent 125 inches long. If the tide rises at a rate of 15 inches per hour — a solid pace I'll grant you — then how long will it take for the water to reach the top rung?"

ROAMERS 98 Solution on page 200

1,434 MILES:

PART 3

The truck was idling somewhere between Livingston and Moundville, but given the uniformity of the landscape and the absence of either the living or the dead they could have easily been anywhere in central Alabama. The air conditioning had gone the way of the world several counties back, leaving the trio one ill-advised comment away from a full-blown argument. Eugene took this as a signal to address Abraham and Rosita, saying:

"It is indeed humid. If I am sure of anything in this life it is that I would be currently willing to enter a shower block populated solely by Alabamians of the cadaverous persuasion, and I say that as a person who is decidedly uncomfortable both with death and the prospect of communal nudity. Nevertheless I have devised a conundrum to test your intellectual fortitude. Try to visualise the field over there being populated with skin eaters. Two thirds of them have lost arms, three fourths possess holes in their stomachs that you can see right through and four fifths have been disabused of their feet. At least twenty six of them have suffered all three calamities, so how many are in the field? Be assured that this is a purely hypothetical situation, although I admit that uttering it aloud means that I am tempting fate."

Solution on page 200

99

ROAMERS

PART 4

Abraham, Eugene and Rosita were approximately ten minutes away from the event that would change their lives forever, but in the meantime they were arguing about pasta. As Glenn and Tara fought walkers down the road, Eugene offered an elaborate tinned food-based scenario:

"I was looking to cross a ford one day and met a strange figure cloaked in black. If either of you had been gamers this occurrence would seem less outlandish. At the time I had come into possession of a quantity of canned pasta in tomato sauce, and he told me that each time I crossed the river the number of cans I had would double. As I was about to thank him kindly he asked for a reward: it would only be fair, he argued, for me to give him eight cans each time I crossed. Being a reasonable individual I accepted and crossed the river. Upon stepping onto the opposing bank I was pleased to discover that he had been a man of his word, and my haul of cans had doubled. I threw eight to the man and decided to cross back over. The number of tins doubled once more and I paid him again. However, I still needed to complete my original objective of getting to the other side of the river, and so I crossed over a third time. The cans doubled in quantity but I realised, entirely too late, that I had been foolish and only had eight cans remaining. After throwing these to the gentleman I was left with nothing but hunger pangs and a bruised ego."

Q How many cans did Eugene have when he first met the man?

Once again Beth saw proof – where absolutely no more was needed – that the world had turned on its head: the prison was like a hospital and the hospital was like a prison. The youngest Greene sister knew that she would find a way out of Grady Memorial if it was the last thing she did, but her goal was aided significantly by Noah commandeering the floor plans. If only they could figure them out.

Q How can Beth and Noah escape the hospital?

The relief of Grady Memorial's newest patients soon turned to despair as they learned that "working off their debt" meant they had essentially been enslaved. Noah, Arthur, John and Percy held different positions in the hospital, acting as – not necessarily respectively – porter, cleaner, cook and Dr Edwards' assistant. Their only respite from indentured servitude were the brief spells when they were able to play cards together; the men were stunned by how something so small could become so meaningful to them, but it was just about the only part of their lives where they weren't actively afraid.

After a few weeks at the hospital some facts became apparent. Both Dr Edwards' assistant and the porter were better card players than the cleaner. Although the porter consistently defeated him, the cook wouldn't play with anyone else. John was worse at cards than Arthur. John and Percy had adjoining quarters and often played together in the evening after their shifts. The cleaner's room was near the cook's but none of the others.

Q What role did each patient hold?

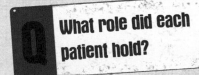

On balance Olivia felt that her life had changed the least out of anyone in Alexandria. Once, she had worked in a coffee shop, now she ran the pantry and armoury. When you were doing a stock take there wasn't a huge amount of difference between a rifle and a muffin. This, unfortunately, made it even harder to resist old habits which once had far less destructive consequences.

It was an open secret that Olivia had been helping herself to Alexandria's supplies. She used a rigorous system to justify the edible embezzlement, pocketing exactly a tenth of all of the food that was requested, but the only person this was fooling was Olivia herself.

Denise had one box of vegetables after the "toll" was taken.

Q How much food did she request?

80 THE QUIZZING DEAD:

1. WHY DOES BOB START LAUGHING HYSTERICALLY WHEN HE DISCOVERS THE CANNIBALS HAVE EATEN HIS FOOT?

2. THE ALEXANDRIA SAFE-ZONE IS RUN BY DEANNA MONROE. WHAT USED TO BE HER JOB?

3. BEFORE ABRAHAM TAKES OVER, WHO WAS THE ORIGINAL FOREMAN OF ALEXANDRIA'S CONSTRUCTION CREW?

4. WHAT WAS WRITTEN ON THE SIDE OF GABRIEL'S CHURCH?

5. WHO DOES DEANNA ENLIST TO BE ALEXANDRIA'S CONSTABLES?

6. FROM SEASON 5 ONWARDS WHAT IMAGE ACCOMPANIES NORMAN REEDUS' NAME IN THE CREDITS?

7. WHAT DOES THE GROUP FIND IN THE MIDDLE OF THE ROAD WITH A NOTE READING 'FROM A FRIEND'

8. WHY DOES CAROL ASK SAM TO STEAL TWO BARS OF CHOCOLATE FROM OLIVIA?

9. IN THE EPISODE 'THEM', WHICH CHARACTER CLAIMS 'WE ARE THE WALKING DEAD'?

10. WHO SECRETLY VISITS DEANNA TO WARN HER THAT THE GROUP CAN'T BE TRUSTED?

 **ROAMERS**

 104

Solution on page 202

THE QUIZZING DEAD:

1. IN SEARCH OF SANCTUARY, THE GROUP TRAVEL TO NOAH'S FORMER HOME. WHERE DID HE LIVE?

2. WHAT MISDEMEANOUR DOES JESSIE ASK RICK TO INVESTIGATE?

3. WHICH THREE MEMBERS OF SEASON 5'S REGULAR CAST ALSO STARRED IN THE CRIME DRAMA THE WIRE?

4. WHAT DOES DR STEVEN EDWARDS KEEP IN HIS OFFICE THAT HE FOUND ON THE STREET?

5. WHERE DOES RICK HIDE HIS GUN BEFORE THE GROUP ENTER ALEXANDRIA?

6. WHAT OBJECT DOES SHELLY NEUDERMEYER DESPERATELY WANT THE ALEXANDRIA SCOUTS TO FIND FOR HER?

7. WHAT DOES AARON CALL THE HORSE HE'S BEEN TRYING TO CATCH FOR MONTHS?

8. WHEN EUGENE IS ACCUSED OF SPORTING A MULLET, WHAT DOES HE DESCRIBE IT AS INSTEAD?

9. WHAT DOES CARL GIVE TO MAGGIE AFTER BETH DIES?

10. WHAT IS PAINTED IN BLOOD ON THE SIDE OF THE CHURCH BY GARETH AND LATER STAMPED ONTO RICK'S HAND BY SAM?

Solution on page 203

105

ROAMERS

PART 1

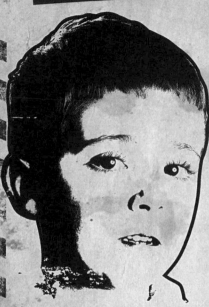

"There is a word for you Sam, and that word is pest", Carol announced to the young boy. Wielding the limitless patience that can drive any adult to madness given enough time, he'd visited every day in the indiscriminate hope that she might give him some cookies. To Carol's general dismay, she'd become the nearest thing to a sweet shop in Sam's cloistered post-apocalyptic life.

Carol had attempted several methods to dissuade the boy including curtness, insults and threats of ghastly chores, but nothing landed. Following a tip from Deanna, she learned that he could be distracted with what he called "scratch-headers". Magnificently, he disappeared for a whole afternoon when she asked the following:

"I have a room in my house where I deal with pests like you. It only has two exits: one leads into my collection of pet roamers, and the other leads into a room that is actually one big magnifying glass, which will toast you if you so much as step into it. How do you escape?"

Q What answer did Sam give when he came running back that evening?

ROAMERS

Solution on page 203

PART 2

Carol was quietly one of Alexandria's finest strategists, but her plan to distract Sam backfired spectacularly. Not only did he now come to her house every day asking for cookies, but he also incessantly demanded scratch-headers too. She was almost tempted to try to deflect him with something else – ironing her clothes, maybe, or cleaning out the guttering on her roof – but he'd inevitably just end up getting obsessed with that too.

With a couple of years of expertise in the subject, Glenn was a reliably useful source for riddles, but Carol preferred it when she came up with them by herself. It was entirely too hazardous to disclose this to Sam, of course, but she was genuinely proud when he arrived at her doorstep and she bamboozled him with:

"Which word does not belong in the following list: Day, Say, May, Flay, Stray, Way, Pay or Bray?"

Solution on page 203

107

ROAMERS

The walls wouldn't hold for much longer. If Rick didn't take action soon, there wouldn't be much of Alexandria left to save: he had learned – the hard way – that things can always get worse.

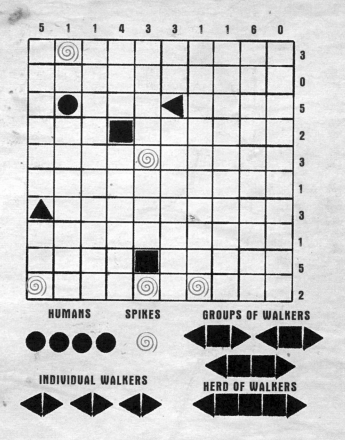

Identify the exact locations of the walkers and humans hidden in this image. All are positioned horizontally or vertically, and no-one is immediately adjacent to anyone else, including diagonally. The row and column numbers indicate the total segments in their corresponding lines.

ROAMERS

108

Solution on page 204

Aside from gunfire and hard objects thumped against their heads, the greatest threat to a walker is their tendency to get ensnared by straightforward physical geography.

Such an event occurred just as autumn started to buffet Virginia. A walker had been shambling towards the distant sounds of Alexandria when it fell into a ditch, twelve foot deep. At the end of the day it had dragged itself up four feet, chomping all the while, but that night it rained and the wretch was carried back three feet.

The walker once had the misfortune of being a hospital porter bitten by a patient – now it had the misfortune of being stuck in a hole during late September in Virginia. Each day it crawled up four feet before the nightly rain swept it back three feet.

Q How many days did it take the walker to escape the ditch?

Solution on page 205

109

ROAMERS

86 A CLEAR OUT

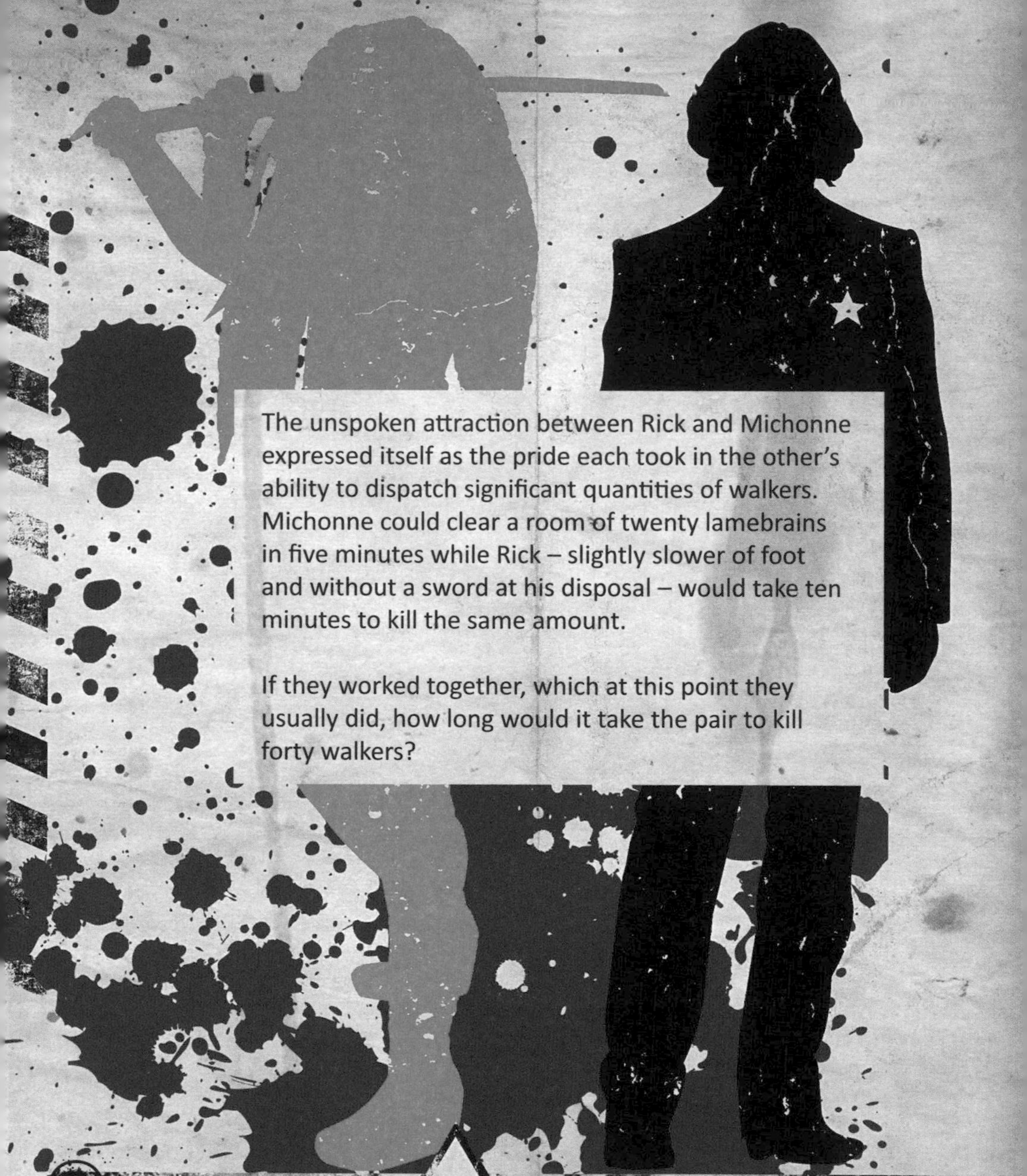

The unspoken attraction between Rick and Michonne expressed itself as the pride each took in the other's ability to dispatch significant quantities of walkers. Michonne could clear a room of twenty lamebrains in five minutes while Rick – slightly slower of foot and without a sword at his disposal – would take ten minutes to kill the same amount.

If they worked together, which at this point they usually did, how long would it take the pair to kill forty walkers?

Solution on page 205

Which Walking Dead character is concealed below?

	1	1	1	1	1	1	1	1	1	1	1	1 3 4	1 8 6	1 2 13	1 6 13	21	3 19	2 18	7 7	3 7 1 2 4 5	1 6 2	3
1																						
21																						
4																						
2 3																						
3 3																						
6 2																						
6 3																						
1 7																						
2 7																						
2 5																						
8																						
7																						
7																						
6																						
5																						
5																						
6																						
7																						
8																						
9																						
9																						
10																						
4 5																						

To reveal the picture, shade the grid's cells so that each column and row has continuous shaded blocks of the lengths indicated by the numbers at the start of that column or row, with at least one empty cell between each block.

88 TENDING THE FLOCK:

PART 1

Before he left them all for dead, Father Gabriel was well liked by his congregation. He livened up his sermons by introducing fun problems, or at least he thought they were fun – his parishioners were more charmed by how fantastical they were. For instance, in one address about the dangers of worshipping false idols, he said:

"It is easy to be fooled, to find yourself following the wrong thing for the wrong reasons. Let's say you see me tomorrow out there on the lake, sauntering without a care in the world. The lake isn't dry, and yet every one of you watches as I walk on water. If your eyes aren't deceiving you, and they're not, then I must be the messiah, right? There can't be any other explanation".

Q In Gabriel's story, how was he able to walk on water?

ROAMERS 112 Solution on page 207

89. TENDING THE FLOCK:

PART 2

Father Gabriel's congregation appreciated the efforts he went to in constructing his sermons, but periodically the message would get lost in the syntax. On one memorable occasion he got himself worked up into a state for reasons that no-one could quite follow, before tossing his bible to the floor and yowling:

HOLY BIBLE

"THE ANSWER I GIVE IS YES, BUT WHAT I MEAN IS NO!"

Q What was the question?

Solution on page 207

113

 ROAMERS

PART 3

In retrospect Gabriel's final address was overshadowed by the fact that he would soon betray his flock and fail to prevent their deaths, but until that point everyone could agree that he had given an excellent homily. The theme, awkwardly enough, was personal responsibility, and as usual he had opened with a riddle:

"Let me tell you about a man that you should aspire to be like. This man was found in the desert, but unlike our lord he did not survive his experience there. His body was discovered naked and battered and he was clutching half of a toothpick. There were no tracks or footprints around him, and his clothes were found a short distance away. Can anyone tell me what happened to him?"

90 TENDING THE FLOCK:

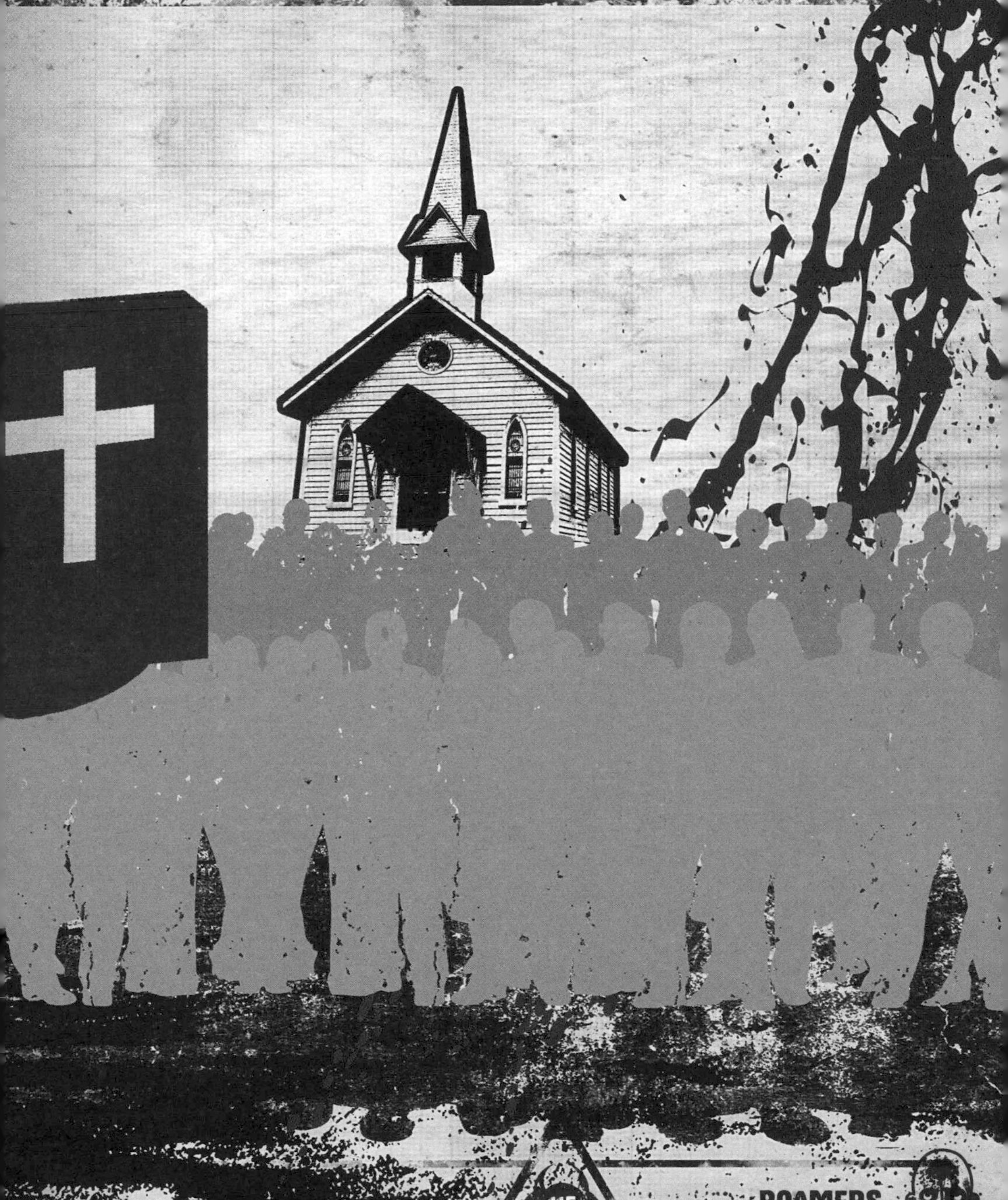

SEASON 6

COLD BODIES

"SORRY, I WAS AN ASSHOLE" said the map, **"COME TO WASHINGTON. THE NEW WORLD'S GONNA NEED RICK GRIMES."**

Morgan was inclined to believe this was a sign, and not only because he found the map in a church, immediately after praying. He would follow its directions all the way to Rick, but first he needed to follow them out of this neighbourhood.

START

PART 1

One unexpected repercussion of the end times was that it revealed talents that had previously lain dormant. It became apparent that if Glenn truly had a gift for anything it was cheating death. Without even taking into account the world being annexed by the undead, the man had survived cannibals, a plague, acting as bait for a floater in a well, being shot by a new colleague and having a walker set on him while he was tied to a chair. And these were only the things he could remember off the top of his head.

Despite his tendency to lurch into life-threatening situations, Glenn was remarkably upbeat. Once a week, without fail, he would surprise his wife with a riddle, and once a week, without fail, she would curse that she had married such a daffy, apparently unkillable man. Maggie's only hope was that sometimes he seemed to be running out of energy – his latest riddle was the silliest yet:

"Which side of a cat has the most fur?"

Solution on page 209 **COLD BODIES**

PART 2

Glenn found it disconcerting how much of his adult life was spent coming up with riddles, but as long as they continued to make Maggie smile, groan or punch him in the shoulder he wouldn't stop. The process was definitely getting more difficult, however: once he gave her the riddle **"What is full of holes and yet holds water?"** only for Maggie to inform him that he'd already done that one back on the farm. Neither could remember the answer, though, so he added a second for good measure: **"Why can you never expect a fisherman to be generous?"**

PART 1

Morgan had chosen an inconvenient time to stop killing people, although perhaps there were no more convenient times left. The Wolves had been stalking him for miles – they wanted everything he had, they said, every last drop.

At some point the Wolves had managed to overtake him, but instead of attacking again they were manoeuvring him somewhere. It was pack behaviour, Morgan supposed. He first became aware of this when he came to some defaced signposts at a fork in the road.

The first path's sign read: **"You should not come this way".**

YOU SHOULD NOT COME THIS WAY

The second path's sign: **"This is the path to take, or else the third path is the correct one".**

The third path's sign read: **"We are waiting for you on the first path, Morgan".**

Morgan knew the Wolves, were toying with him, so he assumed that at least one of the signs would be false.

WE ARE WAITING FOR YOU ON THE FIRST PATH, MORGAN

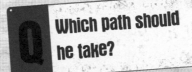

Q Which path should he take?

PART 2

The Wolves were pushing Morgan deeper and deeper into the woods. His progress was slowing: he knew the way back to Terminus but not the way forwards. As he approached another split in the road he saw that the Wolves had knocked down its multi-pronged signpost. The theatricality of it all felt like something from a fairytale: like all Wolves, they were fantasists.

Q How can Morgan find the right road?

PART 3

The longer you lived in this world, the better you became at detecting traps. Morgan knew he was walking straight into one, but he also knew that he could fight his way out. Better to get it over with than to continue being the plaything of men with letters carved into their heads. He approached another divergence in the woods.

Once again, each of the three paths had its own signpost. He'd started to get the hang of the idea, and understood that at least one would be telling the truth and one would be lying, and just one of the paths would be safe.

YOU DEFINITELY SHOULDN'T GO DOWN THE SECOND PATH

The first signpost read: **"You definitely shouldn't go down the second path"**.

The second signpost read: **"We are waiting on this path, Morgan, just out of sight and ready to kill you"**.

The third signpost read: **"This way is safe. We're not on this path. For the love of god, come this way"**.

Q **Which way should Morgan go?**

Solution on page 210 123 **COLD BODIES**

PART 4

The Wolves were unfortunate in their timing: if they'd sprung such a disorientating series of problems even a few months earlier it might have nudged Morgan over a precipice, never to come back. Instead, their opponent was clear-headed and driven by a considerable purpose: he would find his friend again and shake his hand. Morgan smiled as another fork in the road grew closer: they were clearly giving him everything they had. It was their final shot, short of trying to kill him. He assumed that was the next step, of course, but he was ready for that too.

The first path's sign read: **"We'll shoot you if you come this way"** and **"The safe road will pass by a creek"**.

The second path's sign read: **"We'll shoot you if you go down the first path"** and **"The safe road will not pass any water at all"**.

The third path's sign read: **"This road is absolutely not safe"** and **"The second path is really the safe one"**.

Morgan was an old hand at this by now: surely each signpost would contain no more than one false statement.

THIS ROAD IS ABSOLUTELY NOT SAFE

Q Which road should he take?

COLD BODIES   124   Solution on page 210

"**Strongman or wait, you can't break a Rickard Safe**" promised the company's unwieldy advertising slogan, but a more accurate description would have also added "**unless you can figure out the code on its keypad, which is not an unreasonable proposition**". To the delight of survivors across Georgia, those who solved the safe override puzzles were dependably rewarded for their trouble with firearms and rare baseball cards.

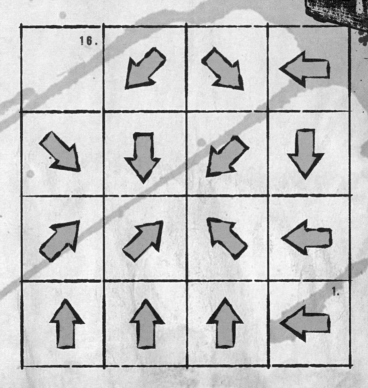

To unlock the safe, move from bottom right to top left, stopping on each square exactly once. The arrows in each square show which direction you must move in.

ALEXANDRIA

Carl had an eye for Enid, that much was obvious. It was bad enough that his father had murdered Ron's, but now he was brazenly pursuing the grieving boy's girlfriend as well. At first Ron was unsure about how to proceed beyond passive aggression; with a couple of years of Alexandria schooling on his former friend, the only plan he could formulate was demonstrating to Enid that he was intellectually superior. He approached the pair in the middle of the street and said to Carl:

"What's four times three times two times one times nothing times one times two times three times four?"

The scheme was a failure: Carl and Enid just walked away as if he'd said nothing at all. Tears burned down Ron's cheeks as he resolved that he wasn't going to let Carl get away with this, or with any of it.

Q If Carl engaged with Ron, what answer should he have given?

100 THE QUIZZING DEAD:

1. WHERE DO RICK AND MORGAN DISCOVER A LARGE GROUP OF WALKERS?

2. HOW DOES GLENN SURVIVE THE GROUP OF WALKERS THAT KILLS NICHOLAS?

3. WHAT DOES AARON COLLECT?

4. WHAT WAS THE HILLTOP BEFORE IT WAS TAKEN OVER BY FEMA DURING THE WALKER OUTBREAK?

5. WHAT DOES MAGGIE SPOT THAT LETS HER KNOW GLENN IS STILL ALIVE?

6. ON HER JOURNEY TO ALEXANDRIA, WHAT ANIMAL DOES ENID EAT TO SURVIVE?

7. WHAT MARTIAL ART DOES MORGAN LEARN TO USE INSTEAD OF KILLING?

8. HOW DOES CARL LOSE HIS RIGHT EYE?

9. WHAT JOB DID GLENN HAVE BEFORE THE WALKER OUTBREAK?

10. WHO IS THE LEADER OF THE WOLVES?

Solution on page 212

127

COLD BODIES

THE QUIZZING DEAD:

1. WHAT BOOK DOES EASTMAN GIVE TO MORGAN?

2. ROSITA AND ABRAHAM HAVE MATCHING NECKLACES. WHAT ARE THEY MADE FROM?

3. ACCORDING TO THE LIST SHE MAKES IN 'NOT TOMORROW YET', HOW MANY PEOPLE HAS CAROL KILLED?

4. GABRIEL WAS THE PRIEST OF WHICH CHURCH?

5. WHAT ITEM DOES DENISE WANT TO SURPRISE TARA WITH?

6. WHICH BUILDING COLLAPSES IN ALEXANDRIA, CAUSING WALKERS TO ENTER THE NEIGHBOURHOOD?

8. WHAT WAS THE NAME OF THE MAN WHO KILLED EASTMAN'S WHOLE FAMILY?

7. HOW DOES JESUS STEAL RICK AND DARYL'S VAN?

9. WHEN CAROL AND MAGGIE ARE CAPTURED BY SAVIOURS, WHICH ITEM DOES CAROL USE TO FREE HERSELF?

10. WHAT DOES GLENN DO FOR THE FIRST TIME WHEN THE GROUP ATTACK THE SAVIOURS' OUTPOST?

102 THE WRONG MAN:

PART 1

It seemed unlikely that Gregory was much of a reader even before the libraries and bookshops vanished, but if he had been then maybe he would have become familiar with the Peter principle – the concept that managers rise until the point that they are incompetent at their jobs. Along with the death of most of his potential competitors, this ignorance perhaps helped explain how he'd been able to maintain his control of the Hilltop despite his manifest corruption and incompetence.

Gregory's ongoing leadership was truly baffling: soon after he solemnly informed the community that they would all be killed if the Saviours didn't receive half of their resources, it was revealed that this rueful situation had come about because he'd lost a bet to Simon. Groans sighed out across the Hilltop as he described the riddle he'd been unable to solve:

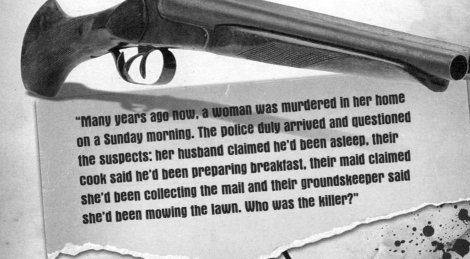

"Many years ago now, a woman was murdered in her home on a Sunday morning. The police duly arrived and questioned the suspects: her husband claimed he'd been asleep, their cook said he'd been preparing breakfast, their maid claimed she'd been collecting the mail and their groundskeeper said she'd been mowing the lawn. Who was the killer?"

Solution on page 213

129

COLD BODIES

PART 2

Instead of ensuring that everyone at the Hilltop had enough to eat, Gregory insisted it would be fairer if people earned food tokens by completing tasks. For reasons known only to him, every resident was also obliged to sign a contract including complicated token-related provisions.

The agreement foisted upon Kal outlined that he would be granted eight tokens a day on the condition that he'd forfeit ten tokens for each day he idled. As a hard worker Kal saw no problem with this arrangement, but soon learned that Gregory's definition of the term was extremely questionable: fighting off a walker attack when you were supposed to be tending a field was somehow counted as idling. At the end of thirty days, Gregory told him that he wasn't owed any tokens, nor did he owe any.

Q How many days did Kal work and how many did he "idle"?

PART 3

With the nationwide electricity grid on permanent hiatus each Virginia community needed to depend upon itself for power. Scavenged solar panels were the obvious solution but Gregory preferred to use wood burners, sending unarmed residents into the nearby forest to chop down trees. When this idea faltered, as it frequently did, the Hilltop was forced to rely on little more than bonfires and a fading sense of optimism.

On one such night, Gregory illuminated his bedroom with a dozen dinner candles in the vain hope that someone might stop by for a romantic visit. Naturally, no-one did. A breeze snuffed out the two candles by the window before dying down for good, and then Gregory fell asleep. How many candles were remaining when he woke up the next morning, cold and alone?

Solution on page 213

 131

COLD BODIES

There are 10 differences between the picture on the left and the image on the right. Can you spot them?

 **COLD BODIES**

 132

133

COLD BODIES

Given the current state of things, it was possible that the fledgling communities could wipe each other out without the aid of a single walker. From Saviour to free man, however, there was one thing that everyone could agree on: Carl's hair was terrible.

It was only after months of teasing from Michonne that the boy capitulated and agreed to take action. Once he finally removed his beloved hat for ten minutes, Carl found that his options were limited. With Jessie no longer available, only two people in Alexandria actually gave haircuts: Glenn, whose flowing locks were generally admired by everyone, and Eugene, whose mullet was so stubbornly dreadful that it was a strange source of comfort.

Q Who should Carl approach?

107 SAFE PASSAGE:

PART 1

"Wait. Not yet."

"Why?"

"There's three of them. Look."

Daryl was right. The house was guarded by three Saviours. They were now huddled together, cradling their weapons and discussing something intently. Aaron raised his parabolic microphone.

"Oh god."

"What?"

"One of them is holding grenades. I'm not sure which."

Daryl studied the expression on his companion's face but couldn't decipher it. He looked to the men as Aaron relayed the information he was hearing.

"Right, so their names are Eli, Roberts and Jim. I believe one is the driver, one is the lookout, and the other has the grenades. They're talking about their youth. Eli was brought up in Connecticut and the lookout was born in Maryland. Jim moved here from D.C. when he was young. They're going on about boxing now: the driver and one of the men originally met at a boxing gym. They're making fun of Jim because he can't throw a punch. Oh, and now they're just insulting each other a lot. Apparently the driver had a bet with Roberts to see who could kill the most 'geeks'. Roberts won. Does that help?"

For a moment, Daryl thought his head was about to topple over, but then realised he knew exactly who they needed to take out first.

Q Which man has grenades?

Solution on page 215

135

COLD BODIES

PART 2

"**The grass is discoloured, see?**"
Daryl nodded towards the lawn. Regular landscape maintenance had slipped down the world's priority list somewhat, but Aaron couldn't deny that something seemed off about the house's back garden. In the middle of its ragged turf was a square patch, slightly lighter than the rest.
"**What does it mean?**"
"**At a guess,**" Daryl said, "**I'd say there's something underneath it. Everything worth having is hidden.**"
It'd explain why the now-dead Saviours had been guarding the house. As Daryl stood watch, Aaron searched the kitchen. It had been barely touched; the cupboards were still stocked with cans of food. He spotted a notebook lying behind some bowls and brought it outside.

"**Look what I found,**" said Daryl.
Near the lawn was a metal box, unembellished except for a numbers-to-letters keypad on one side.
Aaron turned his attention to the notebook, which was similarly blank except for one page. He read it aloud:
"**Shoot at me a hundred times and I may still survive. One scratch from you, and your prospects will take a dive. What am I?**"
"**The answer is the code for whatever this is.**" Daryl suggested. "**It's got to be 'walker', right?**"
"**No, they scratch you!**"
After considering the question for a moment, Aaron crouched and typed a series of numbers into the keypad. Beneath them, the ground began to clank and shudder.

Q **What numbers did Aaron type into the keypad?**

 COLD BODIES   136   **Solution on page 215**

"I know it's odd, but I've always found it a little sad that so many of the survivalists didn't make it," Aaron said. **"Imagine putting years of your life into building and preparing an operational fallout shelter and then getting bit by a roamer on day two, you know? It's called bad luck."**

Daryl made a **"hmm"** sound that generally signified he'd taken in what you'd said but had no intention of responding any time soon. The pair continued to do their stock check. The shelter was filled with non-perishable food, water, medical supplies, rope – almost every type of survival equipment you might need. There wasn't a single open can or empty bottle. It was untouched buried treasure, truly. The only thing spoiling the mood was the dead man slumped over in the corner, holding a gun and a tape recorder. With a quickness that suggested it was an impulse decision, Aaron reached towards the machine and pressed play, the sound blaring out louder than either man had been expecting.

"Sorry. I am sorry," spoke the voice on the tape, **"I guess I couldn't take the end of the world after all."** There was a sigh, followed by the sharp crack of a gunshot, and that was that.

Daryl made his **"hmm"** noise again. Aaron looked to his friend and asked him if he was alright.

"I don't think that man killed himself," he said.

Q **Was Daryl right?**

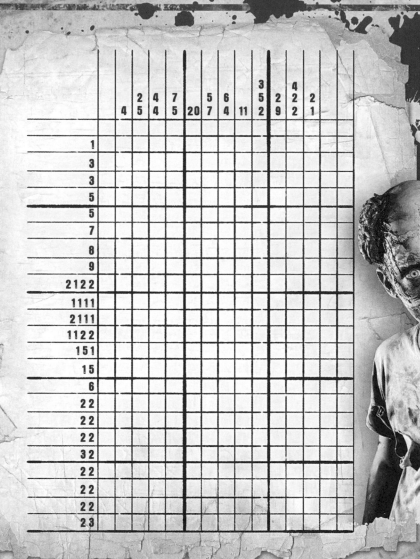

To reveal the picture, shade the grid's cells so that each column and row has continuous shaded blocks of the lengths indicated by the numbers at the start of that column or row, with at least one empty cell between each block.

COLD BODIES

138

Solution on page 216

139

COLD BODIES

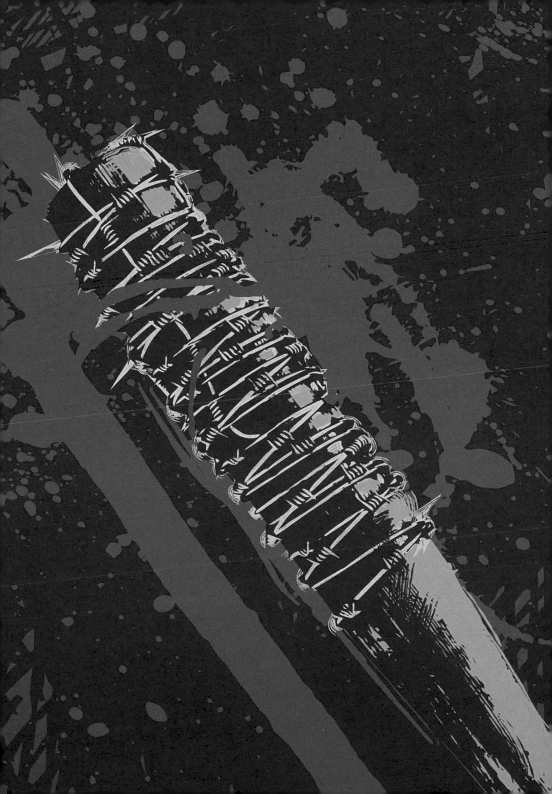

It wasn't Glenn. It was wearing his clothes and his shoes, it had the same arms, the same mole on the same right wrist, but it wasn't him. He wasn't in there. It was just a shape that used to be her husband.

By this point Maggie had seen dead bodies every single day for years, but she was ill-prepared for the moment. It felt worse than if it had happened to her. Unable to bring herself to touch the remains of Glenn's face, she reached instead for the pocket where he kept her father's watch. It wasn't alone, Without even needing to look, she knew exactly what she'd found. Maggie took the slip of paper, held it. Her hands shook from the weight. She unfolded the note and looked at the neat sprawl of Glenn's handwriting. There he was.

> FIRST I AM ONE, THEN I SEEM NONE,
> IN DEATH I BIRTH NEW LIFE.
> WHAT'S RAISED EXCEEDS ME,
> FOR ON BENT KNEE,
> I ADD TO A WORLD THAT'S RIFE.

ROTTERS.

142

Solution on page 217

The Hilltop's elevation usually spared it from walker herds, so the advancing mob meant only one thing: someone was trying to attack them. Sasha looked out at the sea of undead and grabbed her rifle.

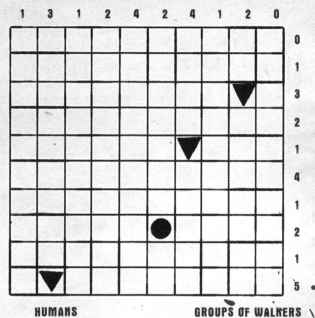

HUMANS

GROUPS OF WALKERS

INDIVIDUAL WALKERS

WALKER HERD

Identify the exact locations of the walkers and humans hidden in this image. All are positioned horizontally or vertically, and no-one is immediately adjacent to anyone else, including diagonally. The row and column numbers indicate the total segments in their corresponding lines.

Being a lookout at night was simultaneously the most crucial and least exciting job in Alexandria, demanding constant vigilance from perils that were hard to spot and that almost never came. Most found the experience agonising, but in its still and silent dells Gabriel found a calm once familiar to him only in church.

Every calm is eventually disturbed, though, and here the cause was three figures, emerging from the tree line. **"Are you armed or not?"** Gabriel yelled, as loudly as a man can when attempting not to wake anyone nearby. The reply from the first man was lost to the breeze, but the second called out **"He says he's armed, but I'm not."** The third man, also referring to the first, added **"He says he isn't armed, and he isn't!"**

In the gloom Gabriel still couldn't see the men well enough to corroborate their statements, but common sense told him that that any armed stranger sneaking around at night would definitely be lying, while it made sense that an unarmed, vulnerable stranger would have a vested interest in always telling the truth.

Q Which of the three men had guns?

It was too reckless to work, too audacious to fail. Faced with a large herd advancing on the railway tracks near Alexandria, Rick and Michonne decided to take an extremely unorthodox approach to the problem. Emboldened by the time they slaughtered hundreds of walkers with just two cars and a tripwire, the pair decided to use a train – an actual, no-fooling train – to mow the whole lot down. The plan was so stupid that it was brilliant.

When one train length away, and travelling at 60 miles per hour, it took the train three seconds to reach the walkers and a further thirty to plough through them completely. How long was the train, and how long was the herd?

Solution on page 218

145

ROTTERS

There weren't many upsides to being ravaged by walkers during your lunch break, but for the employees of Rickard Safes and Vaults one possible consolation might have been that they didn't survive long enough to become unemployed when it was revealed that their safes could be easily cracked by solving a puzzle on the keypad. This company-ending discovery was left instead to the non-devoured contingent of Georgia, who appreciated the steady supply of weaponry that the blunder facilitated.

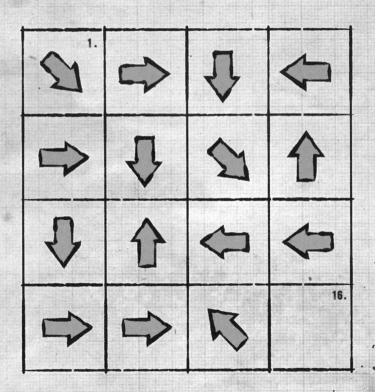

To unlock the safe, move from top left to bottom right, stopping on each square exactly once. The arrows in each square show which direction you must move in.

**ROTTERS**

146

Solution on page 219

PART 1

Richard was ready for a miracle. Stranded in a living hell, wife and daughter both gone, he was desperate to locate some good left in the world, to find something he could believe in. He didn't know what he'd been expecting when he staggered into the auditorium, but it wasn't a man on a throne stroking a Bengal tiger.

"Greetings, fair traveller," said the man. "I am King Ezekiel, and this is my realm. I encourage those who find respite here to enjoy the fruits of our grandeur for as long as they like, so long as they contribute. Drink from the well, replenish the well."

Richard had stopped blinking. This was the first sensible thing he'd heard in months. He tried to nod.

"I am sure that you have been through a myriad of trials, so I beg your patience in asking that you undergo another. This one is less painful, I hope. I'd like to test the mettle of your heart with an enigma, if you'll allow me. Here it is:

'I am born in fear, raised in truth, and I come to my own in deed. When comes a time that I'm called forth, I come to serve the cause of need.'"

Q What was the answer to Ezekiel's riddle?

147

ROTTERS

PART 2

The one sentiment everyone eventually expressed when they got to know Jerry was surprise that someone as nice as him had survived so long. Although this was an ostensibly positive thing, it always felt like an insult. He was so resolutely festive however that he didn't mind.

King Ezekiel responded instantly to Jerry's gentle good nature, but still felt obliged to gauge his moral temperature before he made the man his steward. He did this by reciting the following riddle:

"The beginning of truth, the end of deceit,
The last part of night, as well as of neat.
Turmoil's start and the edge of your seat.
Absent in morals but not so in sleet."

Jerry got distracted halfway through and was unable to solve it, of course, but Ezekiel took pity on him anyway.

Q What answer should Jerry have given?

PART 3

Morgan thought that the man was most likely mad, but maybe that was okay: these were mad times, after all. If everyone you cared about could die and then try to eat you, in that order, then why couldn't a man and his tiger rule a kingdom from a school's amphitheatre?

After polite greetings, a heavily redacted account of his recent history and an offer of apples, pomegranates and nectarines ("**magnificent fruit, grown right here inside the Kingdom**"), it came time for Morgan to be asked a question. "**It may leave you pitch-kettled,**" Ezekiel warned, "**yet a riddle is like this pomegranate: sweet fruit surrounded by bitter. There's something of a contradiction but heaven for the effort.**" The King was florid enough when discussing fruit that Morgan almost didn't notice the question when it appeared:

"**We hurt without moving. We poison without touching. We bear the truth and the lies. We are not to be judged by our size. What are we?**"

Q **How did Morgan reply?**

Solution on page 220

149

ROTTERS

PART 4

There was no light at the end of the tunnel, there was just another tunnel. Carol would have been happy to have been killed by that Saviour, or by a walker, or by absolutely anyone. It seemed lately that the only thing that could make her smile was the thought of no longer being alive, but she couldn't catch so much as a cold. Even after being shot twice she still managed to survive and find herself being offered fruit by a lunatic who was petting a tiger. She was just unlucky, she supposed.

Ezekiel gave Carol his usual spiel and she duly pretended to be the unassuming dormouse that strangers always took her for. She felt like she could see straight through the man, but was surprised to find the same inquisitorial look reflected back in his eyes. He had one more question, he said, and then she could take her leave:

"If a tiger were to say to you that all tigers are lying, would it be telling the truth?"

SEASON 7 EASY

1. HOW DO THE SAVIOURS DESCRIBE THEMSELVES TO DEMONSTRATE THEIR LOYALTY?

2. ON A SUPPLY RUN, TARA MEETS A GROUP OF ALL-FEMALE SURVIVORS. WHERE DO THEY LIVE?

3. WHAT ACTION DOES EUGENE PROPOSE TO FORTIFY THE WALKERS AT THE SANCTUARY?

4. WHEN NEGAN VISITS ALEXANDRIA WHAT GAME DOES HE PLAY WITH SPENCER?

5. WHAT'S THE NAME OF KING EZEKIEL'S TIGER?

6. WHO KILLS SASHA?

7. WHEN THE SAVIOURS TAKE THE SECOND DOCTOR CARSON FROM THE HILLTOP, WHAT DO THEY LEAVE IN HIS PLACE?

8. WHAT DID KING EZEKIEL DO BEFORE THE OUTBREAK THAT EQUIPPED HIM FOR RULING THE KINGDOM?

9. WHAT ARE GLENN'S LAST WORDS?

10. WHICH CHARACTERS WHO APPEARED IN THE SERIES' FIRST EPISODE ARE STILL ALIVE BY THE END OF SEASON 7?

Solution on page 220

151

ROTTERS

SEASON 7 HARD

1. WHAT IS THE FIRST THING THAT ABRAHAM DOES WHEN HE'S 'CHOSEN' BY NEGAN?

2. WHAT NICKNAME DOES EUGENE GIVE TO THE TOY HE TAKES AT THE SAVIOURS' MARKETPLACE?

3. WHO DOES DARYL KILL TO ESCAPE THE SANCTUARY?

4. WHEN SASHA IS CAPTURED BY THE SAVIOURS, WHAT MEAL DOES NEGAN BRING HER?

5. AFTER DECIDING THAT GIN, HIS PREVIOUS FAVOURITE, 'SEEMS LIKE TURPENTINE', WHAT DRINK DOES SIMON BECOME A FAN OF?

6. HOW DOES DWIGHT PREVENT DARYL FROM SLEEPING?

7. THE GATES PROTECTING ALEXANDRIA FEATURE A SIGN THAT READS 'WELCOME TO THE ALEXANDRIA SAFE ZONE'. WHAT DOES IT SAY NEXT?

ALEXANDRIA

8. AS OF THE END OF SEASON 7, WHAT IS THE LONGEST-LASTING RELATIONSHIP ON THE SHOW?

9. WHAT DOES DWIGHT LEAVE IN ALEXANDRIA TO TELL DARYL THAT HE DIDN'T BETRAY THE GROUP?

10. HOW MANY MELONS WAS THE KINGDOM SUPPOSED TO DELIVER TO THE SAVIOURS, AND HOW MANY DID THEY DELIVER?

Gabriel vanishing along with most of Alexandria's food and weapons certainly didn't look great. In the past Rick would have trusted his bleakest instincts, but if the priest could change then so could he. His newfound conviction seemed to be paying off: at the pond they found footprints, leading off into the woods...

Finish

Start

Help Rick track Gabriel to the junkyard.

Money lost all meaning somewhere around the third day of the outbreak. The point was often lost amidst the carnage, but it was jointly terrifying and exhilarating to realise that it no longer mattered how rich or poor you'd once been. You could not buy your way out of this trouble. The new currency was your ability to survive, and beyond that, items that had real value: food, water and guns.

The road back from Oceanside felt longer than the road to it, chiefly because Tara was now on foot and no longer had Heath for company. She instinctively began fretting as she spotted two men sitting together in the distance. Strangers were almost always a danger now. When the men saw her, though, they cheerfully waved her over and asked if she wanted to join them for lunch. One man had three pieces of fruit while the other had five, and the three of them shared the food equally. As they ate, the men explained that they were childhood friends, heading to Pittsburgh to see if their families had made it.

Tara was touched by their unthinking generosity, and wanted to show her gratitude. As she'd lost her gun a while back, she decided to give the men her eight remaining bullets. With the playful truculence of very old friends they debated who should get what: the man who'd contributed three pieces of fruit felt he should get three bullets and his companion would get five, while the other man thought that would be an uneven split.

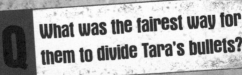

Q What was the fairest way for them to divide Tara's bullets?

Eugene didn't need any outside assistance to be an uncomfortable man; he could accomplish that goal perfectly well on his own. The presence of Negan's wives, therefore, was just an added trial. He felt awkward on several fronts: the women had undoubtedly been coerced into spending their evening with him, one unseemly move on his part would provoke a vicious reprisal from his new overseer, and the one called Frankie was now resting her hand on his knee. Even without the threat of death, Eugene would be petrified. There was surely only one remedy: video games.

Given his capacious intellect and protracted acquaintance with the console gaming scene of the early 1980s, Eugene assumed that victory would come easily. The wives, however, proved themselves to be much tougher opponents than he'd given them credit for, Tanya especially.

A new round of Warlords was about to start. If Tanya lost then she would have won the same number of rounds as Eugene, but if she was triumphant then she would have won twice as many rounds as him. Prior to the start of the new game,

Q How many rounds had Tanya and Eugene each won?

Solution on page 223

155

ROTTERS

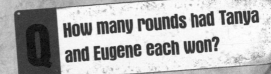

PART 1

Surviving largely means finding something to get you through the day. For Rick, this was his family – he could live off that look Michonne gave him, a smile from Judith, the moments he glimpsed the man Carl was becoming – but as he patted down the dead Saviour, he located something thrillingly tangible. Torn into scraps and deposited across three pockets was an incomplete code. Rick's mind dashed ahead of him: maybe it was the coordinates for another outpost; maybe it detailed Negan's next move. It was enough to see him through to tomorrow, at least.

```
65        7        40        25

    38                56

14        20        1         8


48        12        8         56

    14                 ?

22        24        19        5
```

What number should replace the question mark?

ROTTERS

156

Solution on page 223

PART 2

Rick had become well-acquainted with the pockets of the dead. While Alexandria wasn't quite ready to make its stand, every time he came upon the body of a Saviour – an unsurprisingly frequent occurrence given their tendency to bully others to the point of violent retaliation – he made sure to check each pocket they had.

It was Michonne who finally found Rick's golden ticket, beaming as she returned from a supply run with the second part of the code. It was in one of her pockets, she told him, and if he wanted it then he'd have to look for it...

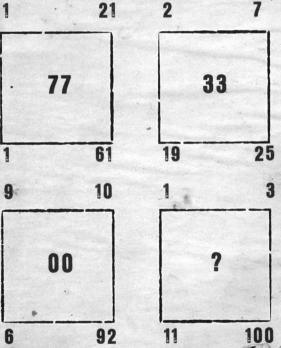

```
  1        21        2         7
 ┌──────────┐      ┌──────────┐
 │          │      │          │
 │   77     │      │   33     │
 │          │      │          │
 └──────────┘      └──────────┘
  1        61       19        25

  9        10        1         3
 ┌──────────┐      ┌──────────┐
 │          │      │          │
 │   00     │      │   ?      │
 │          │      │          │
 └──────────┘      └──────────┘
  6        92       11       100
```

What number should replace the question mark?

Solution on page 223

157

ROTTERS

127 THE SAVIOUR:

PART 1

"Oh Daryl. Daryl, Daryl, Daryl. I know that you think that I'm a bad man. A tyrant. A son of a bitch. Maybe you even think I'm worse than those skin bags out in the yard. But I'm not a bad man, honest to god, I'm a simple one. I'm a simple man with simple rules and if you break them then someone has to pay a toll. This is not difficult to comprehend. When you punched me in the jaw, your buddy had to pick up the cheque, see? It. Is. Simple. Let me tell you a story, and I won't ask for your indulgence because, c'mon,

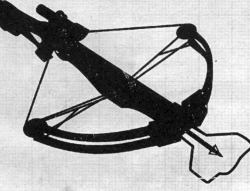

what else are you planning to do today — YOU'RE LOCKED IN A CELL WITH NO NATURAL LIGHT, DARYL — be sensible. Recently one of my night guards came up to me, spooky fellow, he's either a witch or he's from Ohio. This man told me that he'd had a premonition the previous night. He dreamt, you see, that an attempt was going to be made on my life by someone from your sorry crew. And wouldn't you know it, he was actually right! That spooky bastard was onto something. So do you know what I did, Daryl? As a humble token of appreciation, I invited him outside and introduced him to Lucille, and let me tell you, they got on famously. Do you understand why you're hearing this? I am trying to provide you, absolutely free of charge, with some advice. Explain to me, Mr Dixon, why I bashed that man's head into bits?"

ROTTERS

158

Solution on page 224

PART 2

"What has a heart and no other organs, Dr Smarty-Pants?"

"A deck of cards?"

"No, the answer is Rory. Well, maybe there's some of his spleen left."

"If I may be insolent for a moment and ask the obvious question: who's Rory?"

"I made an example of him once, and I guess I'm making an example of him again now, do you get it? OH EUGENE, I AM ON FIRE TODAY! But seriously, don't cross me because you are way too much fun to have around. I would not want to smash that big beautiful melon of yours, and be in no doubt that I would do so without slowing my step. Or maybe I would slow my step a little – like I say, you are certainly dragging some damn fine wagon, brain-wise."

"With all due respect –"

"Yes, that is exactly correct. 'With all due respect, Negan.' You're right to interject, however, I'm not here to have a fireside chat. I need your assistance. I plan to send something to Simon at one of my outposts. You'll understand why I won't divulge what it is – and it definitely is not the actual heart of one of my enemies – using Dwight as a courier. The only problem with this elegant plan is that it's not unreasonable to assume that Dwight could turn heel at any minute and open the package himself, and I don't want to spoil the surprise. I have a box, several locks and their keys, but if I send a locked box to Simon then he won't be able to open it, and if I send a key then I may as well have not bothered at all because Dwight could open it that way. So beyond threatening to burn off the other side of Dwight's face, what can I do to transport this absolutely-not-a-disembodied-human-heart safely to Simon while also allowing him to open it and be totally grossed out?"

Solution on page 224

ROTTERS

PART 3

"Daryl, are you there? What am I saying, of course you're there. If you'd somehow managed to go for a turn around the local park then I would be mightily impressed — mightily Daryl, I mean it — I haven't even visited the park and I'm basically the king of the Mid-Atlantic states. Truth be told I only made it as far as the doughnut shop. It was closed and I was not a happy customer that day, yet you're running around the park like a loyal but not-too-bright dog, so maybe I'm the idiot.

Anyway. Stop distracting me. Something funny just happened, and I don't mean funny like the time I brutally murdered one of your best friends just because you took a swing at me. A person at this facility has been kissing my wife Amber, and I can tell this because when she looks at me there's even more hatred in her eyes than usual. So me and Lucille, armed with this information, rounded up some suspects, and what do you know they started to freak out. I mean really freaking out, Daryl, it was embarrassing. Have a little self-respect when you're about to be executed! Your friends Eyeballs and Moustache did, right?

I start waving Lucille around and some very interesting comments are brought to my attention. Dr Carson jumps in straight away and says that it wasn't him, it was Fat Joey, and then — maybe the fat has somehow got to his brain — Fat Joey says that Dr Carson didn't do it and it was Gavin. No-one had asked Gavin a question at this point, but he then said that Fat Joey didn't do it and it was him that kissed Amber. I thought it was over, praise the heavens and Negan, but James didn't want to be left out and declared that Gavin was innocent and Dr Carson was the guilty kissing culprit. Understandably, I'm now at a loss. I'm sure every one of these morons said something true and something false because they were just so goddamned bug-eyed about it. Like your pal, remember him?

Daryl, you're just about the only person it couldn't have been, unless you took her down the park, so tell me: who kissed my wife?"

Rick Grimes still believed that the world held the means for joy. They'd fought and won. The Saviours had retreated. The Kingdom and the Hilltop had stood with them, shoulder to shoulder, as allies and friends. Yes, there would be other fights on other days, and they would not always be so lucky. There was worse to come, but also better, too. Alexandria had not fallen yet.

It was time to say goodbye. Maggie was needed back at the Hilltop; they were just getting started. She gave Rick one last hug, smiled, and punched him in the shoulder.

"Hey Rick?"

"Yeah?"

"What can't you see that is always before you?"

Solution on page 224

ROTTERS

TURN BACK: PART 1

Rick should brave the highway. If the left or right path is the safe route, all three signs are true, while if the highway is the correct route, all three signs are false.

TURN BACK: PART 2

No, he would fall short. As Rick was driving at 30mph, each hour he was using 1.5 gallons of gasoline and leaking half a gallon, making a total of 2 gallons lost each hour. With his 10 gallons, Rick could only travel for 5 hours before stopping and, at a speed of 30mph, he could only make 150 miles.

TURN BACK: PART 3

"Saddle."

SUPPLY RUNNER RUNNING

Start

Finish

FURTHER DOWN

It's impossible to dig half a hole; if you stop halfway through, it's just a hole.

A PICK OF BAD CHOICES

Carl should select the room that holds the tiger, as it will have starved to death.

SOMETHING HIDDEN

A bloody handprint.

		2	2	1	1	2	5 3	9 5	12	10	2 4 3	8 3 3	2 6	9	3 6	4 3	3	2	1	1
111																				
1																				
212																				
212																				
211																				
222																				
121																				
211																				
21																				
52																				
71																				
18																				
233																				
233																				
143																				
53																				
10																				
7																				
6																				
1																				

167

NUMBERED DAYS

Dale didn't shoot any walkers on Monday. He then shot 3 on Tuesday, 6 on Wednesday, 9 on Thursday, and a dozen on Friday, making 30 walkers in total.

THE QUIZZING DEAD | SEASON 1 EASY

1. Frank Darabont.
2. Sheriff's Deputy.
3. Duane, Morgan's son.
4. Framed photos and family photo albums.
5. "Dumbass."
6. Frogs.
7. They've been caring for the surviving residents of a nursing home.
8. Shane.
9. Bloody handcuffs, a saw, and Merle's amputated hand.
10. That everyone carries the walker pathogen and will turn into one if they die.

THE QUIZZING DEAD | SEASON 1 HARD

1. "DONT OPEN DEAD INSIDE".
2. Jenny.
3. A baseball bat.
4. King County.
5. A mermaid necklace.
6. Andrea was taught to use wet lures, Amy was taught to use dry ones.
7. Center for Disease Control and Prevention.
8. Candace, Dr Jenner's wife.
9. France.
10. Daryl, Merle and T-Dog.

THE SCENIC ROUTE: PART 1

The group had been travelling for 12 days.

THE SCENIC ROUTE: PART 2

Neither Carl nor Sophia had killed any walkers: zero multiplied by two is zero.

THE SCENIC ROUTE: PART 3

Unfortunately, there is not a clear answer to this question. The statement leads to a reflexive chain: his brother argues that, if Dale wasn't fooled, he didn't get what he expected, hence he was fooled, but equally it could be said that, if Dale was fooled, he did get what he expected, so he wasn't fooled. One key problem is that his brother's original declaration to fool him is ambiguous and, without proper limitations, the vicious circle could go on indefinitely. Perhaps it is better instead to discern what message Dale was conveying to Daryl: the notion that older brothers are capable of a particularly cunning sort of malevolence.

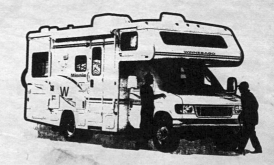

DEAD AIM

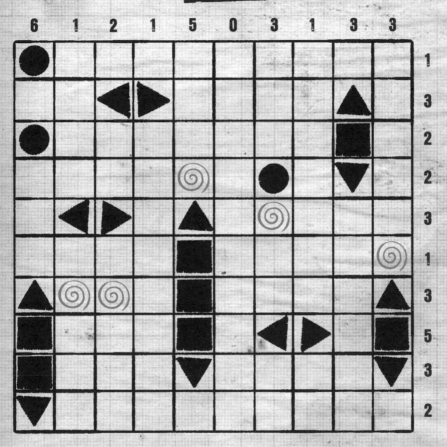

HITTING THE BOTTLE: PART 1

Andrea was the sharpest shooter, followed by Patricia, Jimmy and then Carl.

HITTING THE BOTTLE: PART 2

Beth could give one of the group the crate with a peach in it.

TRACKING GHOSTS

Daryl climbed for 4½ hours and descended for 1½ hours, so it was 6¾ miles to the top of the hill.

SCHOOL ORIENTATION

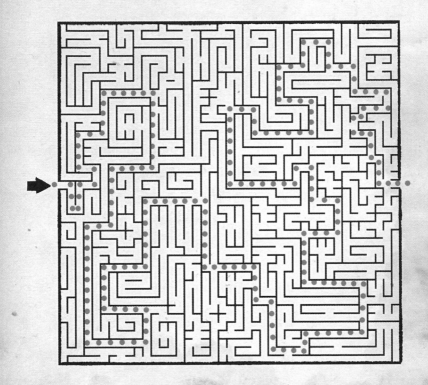

HEALTH PROBLEMS

"You will not give me the silver or bronze medals."

THE QUIZZING DEAD | SEASON 2 EASY

1. Robert Kirkman.
2. She looks down at her map and hits a walker.
3. Otis.
4. A pregnancy test.
5. Dale.
6. To hide that Otis pulled out a chunk of his hair as Shane was killing him.
7. His grandfather's pocket watch.
8. His brother Merle.
9. In the barn.
10. Carl inadvertently causes it to escape the mud bank it was stuck in.

THE QUIZZING DEAD | SEASON 2 HARD

1. "Officer shot".
2. The chupacabra.
3. Nervous Nelly.
4. They're both A Positive.
5. Theodore Douglas.
6. A Cherokee rose.
7. The number 22.
8. Dave and Tony.
9. He falls against a car door.
10. *The Case of the Missing Man.*

MODERN ROMANCE: PART 1

Its shadow.

MODERN ROMANCE: PART 2

Because he has a title.

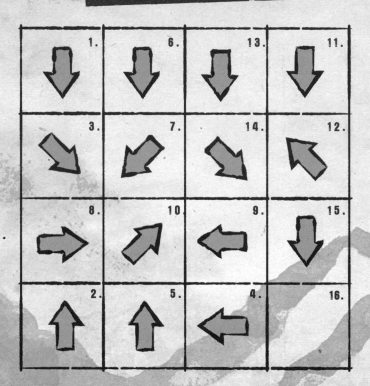

THE LAST FARM: PART 1

Forty posts.

THE LAST FARM: PART 2

The black cows produced the most milk. Treat the first group of cows as 20 brown cows and 15 black cows milked over one day, and the second group as 12 brown cows and 20 black cows also milked over one day. Therefore 20Br + 15Bl = 12Br + 20Bl; so 8Br = 5Bl. It takes 1.6 brown cows to produce as much milk as a black cow.

THE LAST FARM: PART 3

If five people can pack five crates in five minutes, those five people could also pack a single crate in one minute. Therefore, five people could pack 50 crates in 50 minutes.

BAD COP

Including Randall, there were five people in the group.

SPOT THE DIFFERENCE

178

COUNTING THE DEAD

There were 15 walkers in the barn. 3 from Hershel's family, 5 from the next farm, 6 from church and, of course, Sophia.

SOLITARY CONFINEMENT: PART 1

A river.

SOLITARY CONFINEMENT: PART 2

An onion.

SOLITARY CONFINEMENT: PART 3

A cloak.

SOLITARY CONFINEMENT: PART 4

One pours with rain, the other roars with pain.

SOMETHING HIDDEN 2

He is preparing to shoot someone... or something.

Column clues: 1 1 1 2 3 2 1 2 2 3 3 3 3 | 4 1 | 17 22 23 23 | 4 17 16 | 7 2 2 | 6 6

Row clues:
2
4
4
4
5 4
3 3
8 6
13
12
9
7
7
8
8
8
6 1
6 1
6 2
7 1
7 1
6 1
7 1
8 1

A DEATH SENTENCE

The Governor shot Josh.

THE BIG QUESTION

Carol was right: if nothing is better than eternal happiness, and chocolate is better than nothing, chocolate must be better than eternal happiness.

MISSING THE TRAIN

The two trains will be the same distance from Atlanta when they meet.

UNSAFE SAFE CRACKING 2

16.	8. ↘	6. →	7. ←
13. ↓	15. ↖	12. ←	2. ↙
14. ↗	4. →	5. ↑	9. ↙
11. ↗	3. ↑	10. ←	1. ↑

THE QUIZZING DEAD | SEASON 3 EASY

1. Hershel (he has his leg amputated after being bitten).
2. She wants to practise a caesarean ahead of Lori's birth.
3. His undead daughter Penny and three fish tanks filled with walker heads.
4. To retrieve a photograph of himself, Rick and Lori, for Judith to have.
5. Philip Blake.
6. Shane.
7. Michonne stabs him with a shard of glass.
8. Little Ass-kicker.
9. Staged gladiator fights between humans and walkers.
10. Milton.

THE QUIZZING DEAD | SEASON 3 HARD

1. Civil-rights lawyer.
2. His right arm.
3. The Parting Glass.
4. By Big Tiny's count, 292 days; by Axel's, 294 days.
5. A car accident.
6. "Biters".
7. Noah.
8. Cell Block C.
9. "It Could Happen to You".
10. He finds a walker wearing an engagement ring and cuts two of her fingers off.

THE FESTIVITIES: PART 1

Second place.

THE FESTIVITIES: PART 2

Little would also win the second race. At 90 metres, she would be at the same point as Large – both having travelled the same distance as in the first race – and would then be faster in the final stretch.

THE FESTIVITIES: PART 3

Little will lap Large 12 minutes after starting from the same point.

185

THE SLOW ROAD

The pharmacy was 18 miles away from the prison.

If x is the distance between the two places, Daryl rode his bike x/9 hours and walked for x/3 hours, which means $x/9 + x/3 = 8$. Therefore, $x = 18$.

NEW FRIENDS

The Governor had murdered the reservists by putting poisoned ice cubes in the lemonade pitcher. By finishing his drink before the ice melted, The Governor was unaffected.

DEAD AIM 2

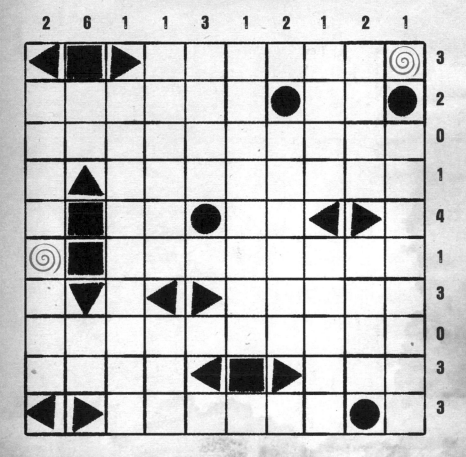

PILLOW PROBLEMS: PART 1

"There".

PILLOW PROBLEMS: PART 2

1. A carpet.
2. Because they don't feel well.
3. Tomorrow.

THE GRAVEYARD SHIFT

Sasha worked from 6 am to midday and from 6 pm to midnight, Maggie worked from midnight to 6 am and from 10 am to 4 pm, Carol worked from 4 am to 10 am and from 4 pm to 10 pm, and Glenn worked from midday to 6 pm and from 10 pm to 4 am.

RETROSPECTIVELY DISCONCERTING

Lizzie is 12 years old.

SPOT THE DIFFERENCE 2

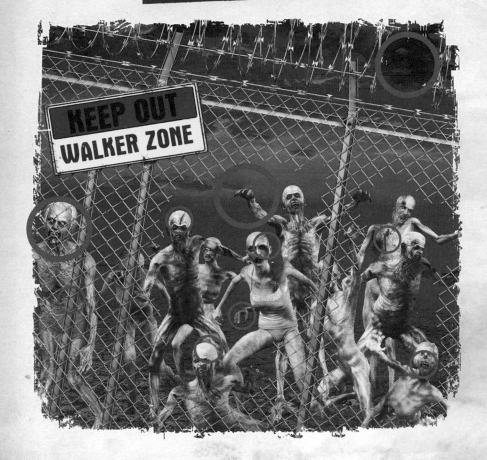

189

THREE QUESTIONS: PART 1

Both women were telling the truth. If the first woman had been a liar, the statement would have been false and so she couldn't have falsely claimed to be a liar. This means that the statement is true and, therefore, the second woman is also not lying.

THREE QUESTIONS: PART 2

Daryl rescued the second man and left the other two behind.

The first man must be lying as, if he wasn't a liar, he'd be telling the truth about being a liar, which is impossible. As he's a liar, his statement is false, so there's at least one non-liar in the group. This means that, if the second man was also a liar, the third man would have to be a non-liar, which would make the second man's statement truthful, and thus impossible. Therefore, the second man must be telling the truth, which means the third man is also a liar.

THREE QUESTIONS: PART 3

Michonne didn't take Edwin back to the prison.

If Amanda had been telling the truth, her statement about Lauren being a liar would be true and, therefore, Lauren's statement would be false, meaning that Amanda and Edwin couldn't be either both liars or non-liars. Therefore, Edwin would be a liar, since Amanda is a non-liar.

From the other perspective, if Amanda is a liar, her statement about Lauren being a liar is false and, therefore, Lauren is telling the truth. If she's telling the truth, Amanda and Edwin must both be either liars or non-liars and, as Amanda is a liar, Edwin must be one too. Regardless of whether Amanda is lying or not, Edwin must be a liar.

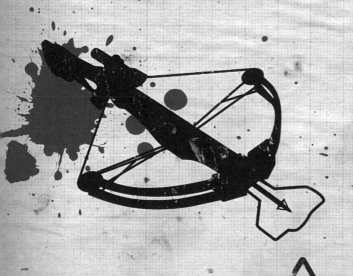

SOMETHING HIDDEN 3

A fire axe.

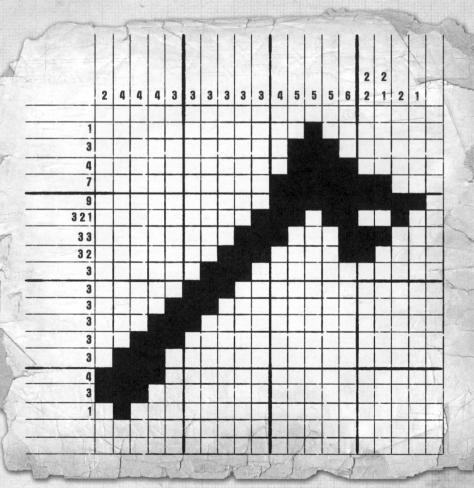

HIS BEST SELF

Daryl had rescued the most people, followed in order by Michonne, Rick and Bob.

UNSAFE SAFE CRACKING 3

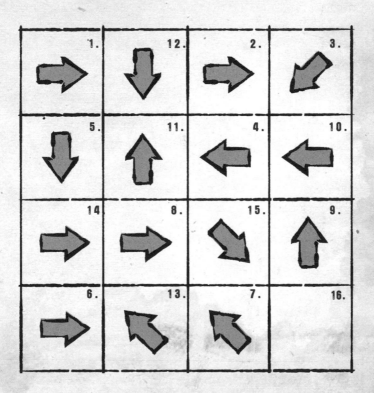

THE QUIZZING DEAD | SEASON 4 EASY

1. Thirty days.
2. How to use knives.
3. "Dr S".
4. A bottle of whisky.
5. Lizzie.
6. A handgun.
7. They are her former boyfriend, Mike, and his best friend, Terry.
8. Hershel, Carol, Sasha, Glenn and Daryl.
9. The Human Genome Project.
10. Hershel.

THE QUIZZING DEAD | SEASON 4 HARD

1. Violet the pig.
2. Oxygen tanks for her father.
3. A 112oz can of chocolate pudding.
4. Homicide detective.
5. A pecan grove.
6. Brian Heriot.
7. Peach schnapps.
8. Griselda Gunderson.
9. Karen and David.
10. Half a rabbit.

SURVIVOR'S GUILT

Other than Bob, the other people in the group were a woman, her daughter and her granddaughter: two mothers, two daughters and three rifles.

BORED GAME

Before they quit, Tara and Lilly played nine hands of the game. First, Tara won three hands, winning three cents. Lilly then won the three cents back with another three hands and, finally, Tara won a further three hands to hold the sum total of three cents. It was unclear what she would spend her winnings on.

JACKSONVILLE, BEFORE

The truck driver was walking.

END OF THE LINE

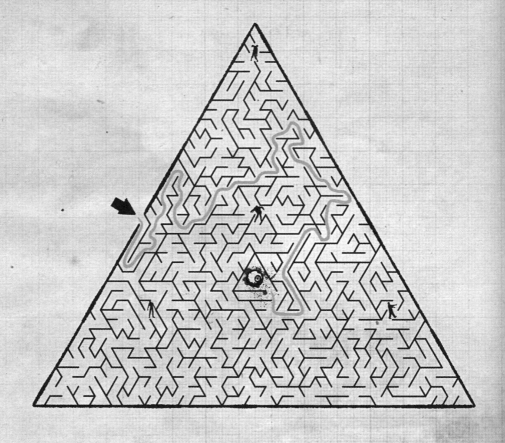

196

HOLDING A TORCH

Yes, the four members of the group could cross the bridge within 15 minutes using a strategy like this:

ELAPSED	ACTION	STARTING SIDE OF BRIDGE	FINISHING SIDE OF BRIDGE
0 minutes		Abraham, Rosita, Rex, Eugene	
2 minutes	Rosita and Abraham cross (2 minutes)	Rex, Eugene	Abraham, Rosita
3 minutes	Abraham returns (1 minute)	Abraham, Rex, Eugene	Rosita
11 minutes	Rex and Eugene cross (8 minutes)	Abraham	Rosita, Rex, Eugene
13 minutes	Rosita returns (2 minutes)	Abraham, Rosita	Rex, Eugene
15 minutes	Abraham and Rosita cross (2 minutes)		Abraham, Rosita, Rex, Eugene

A WAYS AWAY: PART 1

A map.

A WAYS AWAY: PART 2

Stockings.

A WAYS AWAY: PART 3

"When it is put up for a late husband"

WILD CANNIBAL YOUTH

Sasha said "You will boil me in a pot", creating a paradox that prevented the cannibals from taking either action.

MAKING AN EXIT

Instead of tunnelling out, Tyreese plans to dig the earth and pile it up against the wall, continuing until he can reach the window.

UNSAFE SAFE CRACKING 4

1. ↓	6. ↓	4. →	5. ←
2. ↘	11. →	13. ↙	12. ←
9. →	14. →	10. ↖	15. ↓
8. ↑	7. ←	3. ↑	16.

1,434 MILES: PART 1

Eugene claims to be 30, although he is lying about this too.

1,434 MILES: PART 2

The water won't reach the top rung: as the boat will rise with the tide, the water will remain at the same level as the bottom rung.

1,434 MILES: PART 3

As fractions, there are 40/60 walkers without arms, 45/60 with stomach damage and 48/60 with missing feet. If you add together 40, 45 and 48 and deduct twice 60 then the result is 13, which is the minimum number for every 60 walkers. As the minimum who could have sustained all three injuries is 26 then the number of hypothetical walkers in the hypothetical field is 120.

1,434 MILES: PART 4

Eugene had 7 cans when he met the man. As he crossed the ford for the first time this doubled to 14 cans, which became 6 after paying the man. He crossed again and the figure doubled to 12, which became 4 after payment, and then when he crossed for a third and final time his number of cans doubled to 8. He gave these over and was left without any cans.

SLABTOWN

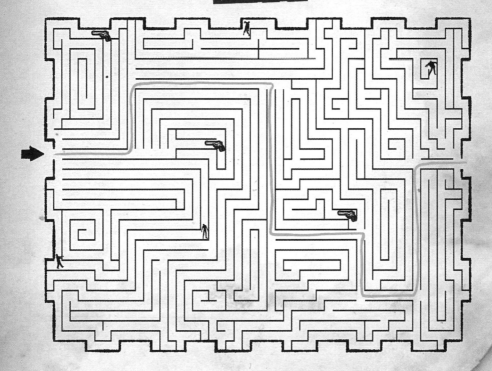

ORDERLY ORDERLIES

Noah was the cleaner, Arthur was the cook, John was Dr Edwards' assistant and Percy was the porter.

STICKY FINGERS

Denise had requested one box of vegetables, plus a further ninth of a box. After Olivia had taken her cut she was left with exactly one box.

THE QUIZZING DEAD | SEASON 5 EASY

1. He was bitten by a walker and so they were eating "tainted meat".
2. Ohio Congresswoman.
3. Tobin.
4. "You'll burn for this".
5. Rick and Michonne.
6. Daryl's angel-wing leather vest, seen through motorcycle spokes.
7. Bottles of water.
8. So she can eat one bar and make cookies with the other.
9. Rick.
10. Gabriel.

THE QUIZZING DEAD | SEASON 5 HARD

1. Shirewilt Estates.
2. The destruction of her owl sculpture.
3. Seth Gilliam (Gabriel), Chad L. Coleman (Tyreese), and Lawrence Gilliard Jr. (Bob).
4. Caravaggio's painting "The Denial of Saint Peter".
5. Inside a blender in the woods.
6. A pasta maker.
7. Buttons.
8. A Tennessee top hat.
9. A music box.
10. The letter "A".

BLOODY KIDS: PART 1

"I will wait until it's night and then leave through the magnifying glass room".

BLOODY KIDS: PART 2

"or".

DEAD AIM 3

Noah was the cleaner, Arthur was the cook, John was Dr Edwards' assistant and Percy was the porter.

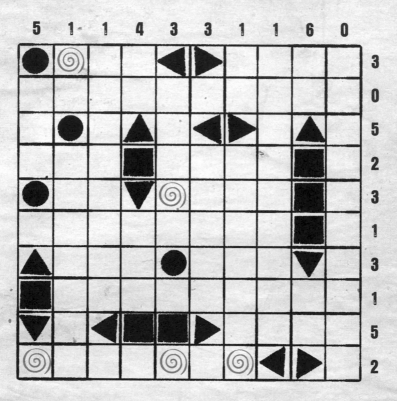

HOLED UP

The walker got out of the ditch in nine days. It was crawling at a rate of a foot per day and night: after eight days and nights it had moved eight feet, and on the ninth day it crawled the remaining four and escaped. Not long after, however, it met Michonne and her sword, and that was the end of the matter.

A CLEAR OUT

It would take Michonne and Rick six minutes and forty seconds to kill forty walkers. Michonne kills at a rate of four roamers per minute, and Rick at the slightly less impressive two per minute.

SOMETHING HIDDEN 4

Michonne.

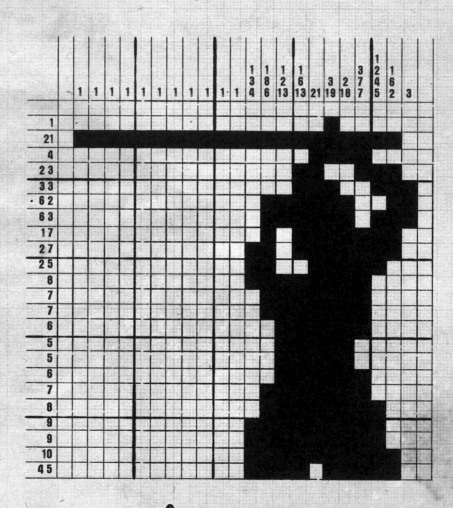

TENDING THE FLOCK: PART 1

It was winter and so the lake had frozen over.

TENDING THE FLOCK: PART 2

"Do you mind?"

TENDING THE FLOCK: PART 3

The man had been in a hot air balloon when the aircraft ran into difficulty. After shedding their clothes, the balloon's occupants found that they were still carrying too much weight, and so they drew toothpicks to see who would sacrifice their life. The man picked the shortened toothpick and consequently jumped to his death.

THE NEW WORLD

LUCK RUNNING LOW: PART 1

The outside.

LUCK RUNNING LOW: PART 2

The answer to the first riddle is "a sponge" and the answer to the second is "because his business makes him sell fish".

WOLVES NOT FAR: PART 1

Morgan should take the first path. If the second or third path is the correct choice, all three signs are true, while if the first path is correct then all three signs are false.

WOLVES NOT FAR: PART 2

As Morgan knows the direction he's coming from he just needs to stand the signpost back up with the right prong facing the way he came.

WOLVES NOT FAR: PART 3

If the third path was safe then then all three signposts would be true, and Morgan knows that at least one is false. If the second path was safe then all three signposts would be false, which is also contrary to what Morgan knows. Therefore the first path must be the safe one – the signposts for the first two paths are true, and the signpost for the third one is false.

WOLVES NOT FAR: PART 4

Morgan could immediately rule out the third path, as if that was the safe one then both of its statements would be false. The first statements on the first and second signposts agree, so they are either both true or both false. If both are false then their second statements would be true, and this isn't possible as their second statements contradict each other. Therefore the first statements for each signpost are true, which means the first road can't be the safe one and it has to be the second one.

UNSAFE SAFE CRACKING 5

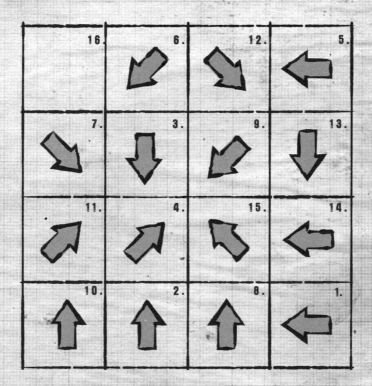

COURTING TROUBLE

The answer is zero: anything multiplied by 0 is 0.

THE QUIZZING DEAD | SEASON 6 EASY

1. A quarry near Alexandria.
2. He hides under a dumpster until they leave.
3. Car license plates from different U.S. states.
4. A museum.
5. Ten green balloons.
6. A turtle.
7. Aikido.
8. Ron shoots him while aiming at Rick.
9. Pizza delivery boy.
10. Owen.

THE QUIZZING DEAD | SEASON 6 HARD

1. *The Art of Peace*.
2. A broken tail light from a car.
3. 18 people.
4. St. Sarah's Episcopal Church.
5. Crush soda (orange flavour).
6. The clock tower.
7. He steals Rick's keys and then distracts the pair with firecrackers .
8. Crighton Dallas Wilton.
9. The sharpened crucifix from some rosary beads.
10. Kill a living person.

212

THE WRONG MAN: PART 1

The maid. She couldn't have been collecting the mail as the woman was killed on a Sunday.

THE WRONG MAN: PART 2

Kal worked for 16 2/3 days and "idled" for 13 1/3 days.

THE WRONG MAN: PART 3

There were two candles remaining – during the night, the ten which hadn't been extinguished all melted down to nothing.

SPOT THE DIFFERENCE 3

A LIFE OR DEATH DECISION

Eugene. As only two people in Alexandria give haircuts, that means that they must cut the hair of the other, so it'd be better for Carl to get flowing locks from Eugene rather than a prominent mullet from Glenn.

SAFE PASSAGE: PART 1

Jim is the man with the grenades.

SAFE PASSAGE: PART 2

Aaron typed in 344482255: the answer is the eightball in a game of American pool, the type enjoyed by Negan.

SAFE PASSAGE: PART 3

Yes, Daryl was right. The man was murdered – if he'd killed himself he wouldn't have been able to rewind the tape. Who killed him and why, however, was a mystery that the pair would never learn the answer to.

SOMETHING HIDDEN 5

A walker.

A SLIP OF PAPER

A seed.

DEAD AIM 4

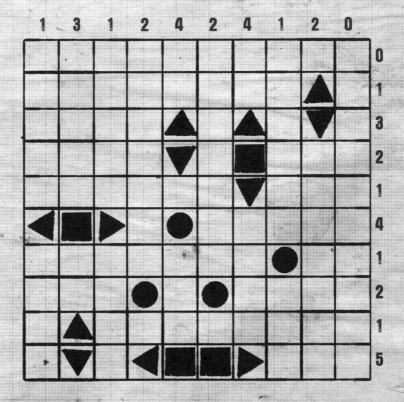

THE SMALL HOURS

The first man, whose response Gabriel didn't hear, could only have said he wasn't armed: if he was carrying a gun he would have lied about being unarmed, and if he was telling the truth he would have also said he was unarmed. The second man then claims that the first man described himself as unarmed, which is a lie, which means that he's armed. The third man is telling the truth when describing the first man, which means that he's also not carrying a weapon. So the first and third are unarmed.

4:30 TO ALEXANDRIA

If the train is moving at 60 miles per hour it is covering 88 feet per second, so the length of train is 88 feet x 3 (seconds), which is 264 feet. To mow completely through the herd the train must travel for thirty seconds, so the length of the herd is 88 feet x 30 (seconds), which is 2,640 feet or 880 yards.

UNSAFE SAFE CRACKING 6

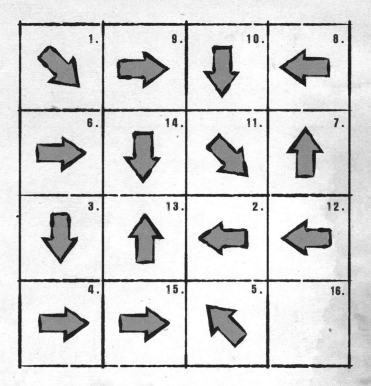

THE WELL: PART 1

Courage.

THE WELL: PART 2

The letter "T".

THE WELL: PART 3

Words.

THE WELL: PART 4

Carol of course replied that tigers cannot talk.

THE QUIZZING DEAD | SEASON 7 EASY

1. They call themselves Negan.
2. Oceanside Cabin Motor Court.
3. Pouring molten scrap metal onto them.
4. Pool.
5. Shiva.
6. Herself, using poison provided by Eugene. After she has turned, Jesus dispatches her.
7. A crate full of aspirin.
8. He played kings in community theatre productions.
9. "Maggie, I'll find you".
10. Rick, Carl and Morgan (Daryl and Carol appear from episode 3 onwards).

THE QUIZZING DEAD | SEASON 7 HARD

1. He flashes a peace sign to Sasha.
2. A grumblygunk.
3. Fat Joey.
4. Pancakes featuring a smiley face made out of blueberries.
5. Tequila.
6. He plays the song "Easy Street" by the Collapsible Hearts Club over and over again.
7. "MERCY FOR THE LOST, VENGEANCE FOR THE PLUNDERERS".
8. Aaron and Eric, who were in a relationship before the walker outbreak.
9. A wooden soldier with "DIDN'T KNOW" written on it.
10. They were supposed to deliver twelve melons but only brought eleven.

AN ABSENT FATHER

STRANGE CURRENCIES

The fairest solution was to give seven bullets to the man who brought five pieces of fruit and one bullet to the other man. A way to comprehend this is to picture the fruit divided into thirds. If each person had eaten a third of each piece of fruit then each had 8 thirds of the total of 24 thirds. The man who brought five pieces provided 15 thirds, so if he consumed 8 thirds himself then he gave Tara 7 thirds. The man who brought three pieces provided 9 thirds, so only gave Tara 1 third. Therefore it is reasonable for the man who brought five pieces of fruit to get seven bullets and the other man to get just one.

WARMONGERING

Before the new game started Tanya had won three rounds and Eugene had won two.

THE HOPEFUL DEPUTY: PART 1

40 should replace the question mark: $(8 + 56) - (19 + 5) = 40$

THE HOPEFUL DEPUTY: PART 2

77 should replace the question mark: $92 - (1 + 3 + 11) = 77$

THE SAVIOUR: PART 1

He was the nightwatchman – by telling Negan about his dream he'd inadvertently confessed to sleeping on the job.

THE SAVIOUR: PART 2

Eugene suggests the following plan: Negan puts the item inside the box and seals it with one of his locks. When Simon receives it he then attaches his own lock and returns it. Negan then removes his lock and sends the package back to Simon, who will be able to remove his own lock.

THE SAVIOUR: PART 3

James kissed Amber. If it was Dr Carson, then James would have been telling the truth about that, but lying when he said Gavin was innocent, which he couldn't have been. Whereas if Fat Joey was the amorous lover, then Dr Carson's statements would follow the same incorrect logic as James's. Likewise for Fat Joey's statements, were Gavin to have been the culprit.

KEEP GOING

The future.